A GIFT

F R O M

THE MIRACLE OF

The Christmas Child

Penelope J. Stokes

J. COUNTRYMAN • NASHVILLE, TENNESSEE

Published by J. Countryman, a division of Thomas Nelson, Inc.,

Nashville, Tennessee 37214.

Project editor—Terri Gibbs

Designed by David Uttley Design, Sisters, Oregon

ISBN: 08499-5420-7

Contents

THE MESSENGER

abriel ducked behind a hay cart and waited until the laughing group of men and women passed by and disappeared around the corner of the synagogue. There was little chance that anyone would see him—people didn't much expect celestial visitors nowadays, and humans couldn't see an angel unless they had their eyes open for one. Besides, he had taken on flesh for this mission; anyone who did see him would probably think him just another traveler, barely worthy of notice.

Gabriel had accomplished this kind of assignment before, but he always felt a little more comfortable in the role of warrior than he did in the garb of messenger. Humans understood battle; they were always more than ready to fight for liberty or conquest. They had a much harder time comprehending the subtler ways of God.

Take Abraham, for example. The Lord's people called him the "father of faith," but he might more accurately be dubbed, "the father of failure." Gabriel had gone to him, too—he was the first, in fact, of this long line leading up to the culmination of miracles in the Messiah. Abraham was nearly a hundred when Gabriel brought him the news that he would produce offspring as numerous as the sands of the sea or the stars in the sky, that he would be the patriarch of a mighty nation bearing the name of the Almighty. Still, for all Abraham's faithfulness in following God, he couldn't seem to grasp the concept of miracle. He went out and had a baby on his own, with his wife's servant—and everybody had been paying for the mistake ever since.

And Moses! Why did humans have such a hard time seeing the big picture? Moses had been called from birth, but he simply could not accept it. Even out in the wilderness, with

...for a brief moment Gabriel wondered if the Almighty had considered all the ramifications of enfleshing the holy in human form.

that burning bush right before his eyes, he argued with God about the Lord's choice of him as the liberator.

Gabriel shook his head. Among his troops, you wouldn't find such insurrection. Rebellion had only occurred once among the angels, and that situation had been dealt with quickly and decisively. But somehow God seemed to be more lenient with these humans, giving them second chances—sometimes even thirds and fourths. The Almighty called it grace. Gabriel wasn't about to dispute the issue with the Lord, of course, but he had to admit that he still didn't quite understand what grace meant.

He suspected he was about to find out.

He looked around and, seeing no other late-night revelers, stepped out into the street. The moon shone full and bright overhead, washing the square around the well with an ethereal glow. Earth was beautiful, even this poor village of Judea, and for a brief moment Gabriel wondered if the Almighty had considered all the ramifica-

tions of enfleshing the holy in human form. It was a great miracle, certainly the greatest the world had ever seen, but it could prove to be a risk. Might not even the Son of God be enthralled by the loveliness of such a moon on such a night, by the vitality of air in his lungs and blood in his veins and power in his muscles? What if he could not bear to give up humanity to fulfill his Divinity?

Gabriel sighed and walked on. It was not his place to question, at any rate. He was only the messenger of this outrageous plan. He was the one charged with bringing the news to God's people: The long-awaited Messiah was about to be born.

The archangel shrugged. He might not comprehend it all, but it was just like God to do this in a

13

way nobody would have expected. The Breath of the Universe would not arrive on earth with pomp and glory and adulation, but as a baby. A squalling, vulnerable, dependent infant. And a poor one, at that.

The Almighty was a master of metaphors, that much was certain. What a picture of God's love—the Divine One becoming human, vulnerable, sharing the secrets and longings of men and women in every generation. Showing the world, face to face, the image of the Creator, the justice and mercy of God. Taking the risk of being rejected.

But who would be so foolish as to reject the Anointed One? Gabriel couldn't imagine that any of God's people, after centuries of praying for a savior, could possibly turn away from him or fail to recognize him when he came.

Oh, no. They would celebrate the announcement. They would believe. They would spread the news. Life on this speck of dust in the universe would never be the same again. The world would embrace the truth with great joy, would cherish the Holy One of God just as Heaven itself cherished him. He could almost hear the celebration in his mind:

Glory to God! The Messiah has come!

How could they do any less in the presence of such a miracle?

top pacing, Zechariah!" Aaron, son of Malachi, grabbed at his arm to slow him down. "It is almost time for the drawing of lots. You'll know soon enough whether you have been chosen to offer the incense today."

Zechariah turned and smiled wanly at the young priest. He looked so much like his father, who had been Zechariah's closest friend and confidant for nearly forty years. Of course the lad would think that Zechariah's agitation stemmed from anticipation over the drawing of the lots. Aaron was full of faith and fire—his whole world centered around the temple, and his service to the Almighty.

Once it had been that way with Zechariah, too. And with Malachi, now dead these thirteen years. As young priests, only a bit more mature than Aaron, they had been humbled and exalted to hold the holy fire in their hands. They were the chosen, the ones who stood before the altar of God on behalf of those who prayed outside. In those days they believed that anything was possible, that the next circumcision to be performed might be the promised Messiah.

But time and age and weariness had taken their toll. Zechariah had stood on the outskirts and watched as Malachi and the other priests brought their sons for circumcision, as the sons grew into men and took their places at the altar. As it should be—as God had intended it to be—sons and grandsons followed in their fathers' footsteps. But there had been no son for him and Elizabeth. No sign of God's blessing upon their faithfulness.

Zechariah was tired, not only with the physical fatigue that accompanied old age, but with a deep-seated exhaustion of heart and soul. For a long, long time, he had managed to find a way to cling to hope—Father Abraham and Mother Sarah, after all, had given birth to Isaac when Sarah was long past childbearing. Might there not be a miracle in store for him and his wife as well? But the years came and went, and there was no child. And at last Zechariah stopped hoping.

With the loss of hope, the spiritual fire within him burned to ash. He would keep on serving God, of course—he was a priest for life. But he could not rid his mind of the overwhelming question: Had he somehow displeased God? Had he not been faithful? There was no other explanation for the emptiness of his wife's womb and the barrenness of his own soul.

A tug on his sleeve brought Zechariah out of his reverie. Aaron stood before him, his bearded young face eager and excited. "The lot has fallen to you, Zechariah. Today you will stand before the Lord in the sanctuary and offer incense unto God."

Zechariah tried to smile, tried to reflect in his own weathered countenance the thrill young Aaron felt on his behalf. He nodded, squeezed the boy on the shoulder, and went to take his place in the sanctuary.

He had been in the holy place many times during his years of service in the temple. But today, something seemed different. A strange illumination cascaded over the altar of the

Lord, and he craned his neck, trying to discern where it came from. Then, out of the corner of his eye, he caught a movement, a glimmer. Had someone invaded the sanctity of the temple? He whirled to confront the interloper, but saw nothing.

There it was again! Right on the edge of his vision! But his eyes were old and often deceived him. He shook his head to clear his mind and proceeded to the altar to offer the sacrifice of incense. Suddenly, from the right side of the altar, a voice spoke.

"Zechariah."

Now he saw it—the vague shape of a man, luminous, as if lit from within by some celestial brightness. He knew, of course, that in the past God had spoken to humans through angels, but he had never seen one, never expected to see one. His ancient knees trembled and almost gave way.

"Do not be afraid."

That's what they always said, according to the Scriptures. Now Zechariah knew why. But the comforting words did nothing to still the pounding of his heart.

"Your prayer has been heard, Zechariah. Your wife Elizabeth will bear you a son, and you will call his name John. You will have joy and gladness, and many will rejoice in his birth. For he will be great in the sight of the Lord—"

The Messiah? The question leaped into Zechariah's mind unbidden. It was presumptuous, of course, but he had to know.

The being smiled and shook his head benignly, and the light within him grew brighter. "Not the Messiah. The one who will prepare the way. Your son will be full of the Holy Spirit, and many will return to the Lord because of him. The spirit and power of Elijah will rest upon him, and he will turn the hearts of Israel back to God and make ready a people prepared for the Lord."

Zechariah sank to the steps of the altar and looked up, incredulous. Could he believe it? Could it possibly be true? A son, after all these years? And not just any son, but a son called by God to prepare the way for the Messiah?

"How will I know this is true?" he asked, half to himself. "I am such an old, old man, and my wife—"

The angel silenced him with a stern look. "My name is Gabriel," he said, his voice reverberating in the very depths of Zechariah's soul. "I stand in the presence of God, and have been sent to bring you this good news."

Gabriel? Zechariah's stomach quivered. Gabriel, the archangel, captain of the Lord's hosts? He held his breath, half expecting to be struck down where he sat.

"My words will be fulfilled," the angel went on. "But because you did not believe, you will be unable to speak from this moment until the day these things come to pass."

Zechariah opened his mouth to reply, to ask forgiveness for his unbelief, to thank the archangel for his message. But no words would come. And then, as suddenly as it had appeared, the angelic vision vanished.

For a long time Zechariah sat on the altar steps, unable to move, his duty of presenting the incense all but forgotten. He closed his eyes, and when he opened them again, the odd light that had enveloped the sanctuary was gone. He must have dreamed it; must have passed out or fallen asleep. An old man's mind plays tricks on him; perhaps, from the last vestiges of his long-held hope, he had simply heard what his soul longed to hear.

With great difficulty, he lifted his arthritic body off the steps and went to prepare the incense. But when he raised it aloft over the altar and began to speak the holy words, no sound crossed his lips. He tried again. The breath was there, and the words filled his consciousness, but his ears heard no utterance.

He could not speak. God would have to hear his heart.

Once more, as he had done since his youth, Zechariah held the holy fire in his hands and made prayers before the Lord Almighty. Tears streamed down his cheeks and fell onto the altar, onto the floor, onto the priestly garb he had worn for nearly as long as he could remember. In silence he prayed on, and as he prayed, his heart grew strong, his soul swelled with thankfulness to the God who had not, after all, forgotten his years of faithfulness.

He was mute because he had doubted, Gabriel had said. He would stay mute until the day of miracle when Elizabeth delivered their firstborn son.

But Zechariah doubted no more. His voice might be still, but his heart shouted hallelujahs. A flame of new life blazed in his soul, nearly taking his breath with the wonder and the glory. And there would come a day—less than a year from now—when he would proclaim the praise of God in the presence of all the people. He would dance like David, sing and leap for joy like Miriam. His sorrow had been turned to song, and his mourning to gladness.

You're never too old to believe, he thought. *Never too old to hope.*

And despite the fact that no sound came, Zechariah laughed.

he old woman sat in the courtyard and watched as the sunrise painted brilliant colors across the eastern sky. Her husband still tossed and snored in the bed they had shared for more than fifty years, but sleep eluded her. Yet it wasn't her husband's restlessness that kept her awake. The truth was, she welcomed his snoring; it was the only sound he was now capable of making, and in the night it reassured her that he was still beside her.

No, her sleeplessness derived from a different source—the deep reservoir of joy and life that stirred within her. After all these years, after all the prayers, after all the anguish and frustration and near despair, at long last, a child filled her womb. A son!

Elizabeth had slept little since the day Zechariah had come home mute from the temple and laboriously written out the story of the angel's announcement. She had never been so glad that her husband had taught her to read. Certainly, she was blessed by her knowledge of the Law, but how much more blessed by this revelation!

She had gone to him immediately, and their love that night reminded her of the passion and glory of their early years together. The very next day, she knew in the way only a woman can know, that she was, indeed, with child. And from that moment on, she had been reluctant to sleep, not wanting to miss a minute of the miracle these six months past.

As the morning light grew stronger, she looked down at her hands, folded in her lap. Ancient hands, spotted with age and crinkled like old parchment. She ran her fingers over her face, tracing the familiar wrinkles that years had left behind. She couldn't deny the truth—she was an old, old woman. But she didn't feel old, not any longer. A new vibrancy coursed through her veins; her step was lighter, her joints more flexible. She felt wonderful, like a young woman again. Instead of waiting for death to claim her, she looked forward to each new day. She daydreamed about the future—what her son would look like, what strengths he would inherit from her and from his father.

Her husband had been adamant—the boy's name was to be John. Elizabeth didn't understand why; there were no Johns in their family lineage. But Zechariah was the one, after all, who had had the encounter with the angel; who was she to question? And if truth be told, she didn't care one bit what the child's name would be; she simply wanted him to be whole and happy and lead a long and prosperous life.

The child kicked within her womb, and Elizabeth's heart leaped with the movement. She laid a hand over her midsection and smiled. "Easy, my John," she murmured, "you'll be out into the world soon enough."

She began to sing to him, the ancient tune of one of David's songs: "Because your steadfast love is better than life, my lips will praise you. So will I bless you as long as I live. . . ."

Perhaps it was her imagination, but Elizabeth thought she felt the child in her womb moving in time to the music. Praising within her, lifting silent hallelujahs to the

Almighty. Without a voice, singing and dancing in worship before the Lord.

But soon enough, he would have his voice. He would be a great man of God, Zechariah had told her, empowered with the spirit of Elijah to prepare the way for the coming Messiah.

But what did that mean? Was he to become a priest in the temple, offering sacrifices and tending the holy fires, as his father had done for so long? Or did God have another calling for her son, something neither of them could yet imagine?

And—the most important question of all—did this mean that Elizabeth and Zechariah would live to see the coming of the Messiah?

It was a question Elizabeth hadn't asked in many years. Every daughter of Sarah prayed that her son might be the Anointed One of God. Elizabeth had held the same hope herself. But it had been so long, and in time the dream had vanished like morning mist on the hills of Judea, burned off by the hot sun of reality.

Now the hope had returned—not only Elizabeth's long-delayed desire to bear a child, but an even greater hope, the anticipation of the promised Savior who was to come. It wouldn't be her John—Zechariah had been very clear on that point. But if John was to be the forerunner, the messenger, did that not mean that the Messiah was, at last, on the way?

Perhaps, at this very moment, some other woman sat in her courtyard and watched the same sunrise, overwhelmed by the glory that had been bestowed upon her. Perhaps Elizabeth might one day meet the mother of the Messiah, and together they could share the wonders of this unexpected grace. But even if she didn't, the bond between them remained. In the meantime, she would pray every day for that woman, and for the child she carried.

23

abriel paused near the well in the square, letting the moonlight spill over his face and chest. Six months had passed since his last sojourn on earth, and he had nearly forgotten how lovely the night could be. Surely the Almighty smiled down upon this glorious evening—the moment when the Blessed One would learn just how blessed she truly was.

Tonight, under this full smiling moon, he had the joy and privilege of making the greatest announcement in the history of human life. Tonight he would fulfill, for one woman, the dream and hope of every Jewish mother in every age. He would tell the Vessel, Mary, that God had chosen her to bear the Messiah.

He hoped she would take the news with more grace and acceptance than Zechariah had. The old man hadn't believed, and now he would have no voice until the Voice Crying in the Wilderness uttered *his* first cry.

Gabriel wondered again why humans had so much trouble accepting the answers to their prayers. They seemed not only determined to tell the Lord *what* to do, but when and where and how. The old priest should have known better; he had served in the House of God all his life. But then, maybe religious activity didn't necessarily correlate directly to real faith.

Gabriel hoped—trusted—that Mary would be different. Gabriel imagined her in his mind—a regal, mature woman, a true daughter of Sarah, settled in heart and soul and fully prepared to take on the awesome task of bearing and raising the Messiah.

The archangel found the house, modest by any standards, and went inside. There, on a grass mat with her eyes closed and her hands lifted to heaven, sat a young girl. Praying, Gabriel thought. A devout daughter of Zion. He smiled, then frowned. Surely this girl was not Mary's daughter—the Vessel was supposed to be a virgin.

The word of confirmation resounded in his mind, and he looked closer. *This* was Mary? Why, she was little more than a babe herself! She couldn't be more than thirteen, in the revolutions humans counted as years. Slim and lithe, with long dark hair and a clear, guileless face, she looked as if she should be out laughing and talking with the other girls. Not preparing herself, soul and body, to bear the Holiest of All.

Gabriel pushed back the questions and doubts that nagged at him. He had a job to do, and he would do it, despite his reservations. He was about to change her life forever, and he could only hope that the change would bring joy rather than sorrow to this lovely woman-child. He took in a breath, infused his human form with angelic brightness, and cleared his throat. "Greetings, favored one," he said. "The Lord is with you. Blessed are you among all women."

The girl's eyes flew open, and she shrank back against the wall. Clearly she was terrified at the apparition before her.

Gabriel's heart went out to her, and he reached a hand in her direction. "Do not be afraid, Mary. You have found favor with God. You shall conceive and give birth to a son, and you shall call his name Jesus. He will be great, the Son of the Most High God, and will rule over God's people forever."

A strange looked crossed Mary's innocent face, an expression of wonder and confusion. "But how is this possible?" she asked. "I have never been with a man."

The archangel suppressed a smile. Leave it to humans to raise the practical dilemmas of

She waited, watching him with wide eyes. She did not ask for proof, or for further explanation. She merely accepted.

life, even in the midst of divine intervention. But he had to give her credit. She didn't argue or protest, the way Moses had when God called him to lead the children of Israel out of bondage. She wasn't trying to figure out a human way to do it, as Abraham did when God told him he was going to be the father of many nations. She didn't doubt, as Zechariah had. She only asked one simple, profound question: "How can this be?"

And he had only one answer: God will do it. "The Holy Spirit will come upon you," he said, "and the child you will bear will be holy, and will be called the Son of God."

She waited, watching him with wide eyes. She did not ask for proof, or for further explanation. She merely accepted.

"Your cousin Elizabeth," he went on, "even now is pregnant with a son. She is very old, and everyone thought she could not have a baby, but she is six months along. With God, you see, nothing is impossible."

Gabriel watched a surge of joy flash in Mary's eyes. She was happy for her cousin's good news—that was a positive sign. The pure of heart can rejoice when others are blessed. But she was young, so very young. How could she bear the weight of such responsibility?

The archangel lifted his eyes to heaven and offered a prayer on her behalf, that God would strengthen her and make her equal to the task that lay before her. Then, as if in answer, a shaft of moonlight pierced through the narrow window and illuminated Mary's face. Bathed in the glow, radiant with heaven's light, she looked as if she herself could be an angel, a celestial messenger charged with bringing good news to God's people. The strong planes of her young face and the determined set of her jaw told Gabriel all he needed to know.

Her age was not important. She had been chosen for her character.

She rose from the mat and flipped her dark hair out of her eyes, then faced him with a clear gaze and a slightly stubborn tilt of her head. "I am God's servant," she said deliberately. "Let it be as you have spoken."

The light from the moon increased and filled the humble room. Mary sank back to the floor, trembling a little when the glory cascaded over her. As the Shekinah of the Holy One descended, Gabriel removed himself from the house. She had responded with an obedience unlike anything he had ever witnessed. It was time to give her privacy in God's presence.

Besides, he had other work to do before he could return to his place near the throne. There was a man to deal with, one Joseph the Carpenter, Mary's betrothed. Only God knew what his response would be when he found out his intended was pregnant.

With another glance at the dazzling moonlit sky, Gabriel made his way through the streets of Nazareth. None of the people asleep in these darkened houses had any idea of the miracle that had taken place this night. But high above them, Gabriel knew, the heavenly chorus was singing hosannas in celebration of the long-awaited Incarnation.

He looked back over his shoulder in the direction of Mary's house. "Blessed are you among women," he whispered into the night air. "I hope Joseph knows what a gift he has been given."

hen the light had dissipated and the messenger had vanished, Mary knelt in the darkness with her head in her hands, weeping softly.

She didn't know exactly why she was crying. Was it that soft, feathery fluttering that filled her being when the light came down? There had been so much love in that moment—a response from within the depths of her soul unlike anything she had ever experienced. Never had she had imagined that she could feel the nearness of the Almighty so palpably, or that her senses could be so full of God's presence.

Was this how Sarah felt when the announcement of Isaac's conception came to her? Or Hannah, with her son Samuel? Or even her cousin Elizabeth, who the messenger had said was also with child? But they were old women, mature in the ways of God, wise and honored. Mary was little more than a child herself, and yet the announcement had come to her, of all people. Her mind replayed the angel's words—*Blessed are you among women.*

The problem was, she didn't *feel* like a woman, not really. She was betrothed to Joseph, of course, and that in itself was testimony to her womanhood. Her pulse quickened every time she saw her intended—that strong, handsome, muscular man who had claimed her for his own years ago. Like all her friends, she dreamed of the day she would cross that threshold and fulfill her calling to become a wife and mother. They all talked about it, giggling behind their hands as they speculated what it would be like to be married. Yet the joining itself was still a long way off, and in her heart she felt like a girl.

She was one of the fortunate ones, she knew. Her father had chosen well for her, a man she could respect and, in time, learn to love. A man of noble character and deep faith. A carpenter, a craftsman whose reputation was known throughout Judea. He would be a good provider—and, she hoped, a loving and tender husband.

Suddenly the truth descended upon Mary like a wave cresting overhead.

Mary and Joseph would be a good match. Everyone said so.

But what, Mary wondered, would happen now? She did not doubt for a moment the truth of the angel's announcement—somehow, by some miracle she couldn't possibly understand, she had been chosen as the Vessel for the Messiah. It was the long-cherished dream of every daughter of Sarah, to bear a son who would become the Chosen One. And now it was happening to her—but not at all in the way she had expected.

Wouldn't someone else have been a better choice? Someone who was older, settled, more mature?

Suddenly the truth descended upon Mary like a wave cresting overhead. *She* had been honored by God to bear the Holy One. She had said yes, and the power of the Most High had come upon her. The glory of the Almighty had overshadowed her. Even now the Child was growing within her, drawing sustenance from her body, being formed in her inward parts. It was done. There was no turning back.

But what would it mean for her life, the plans she had made for the future?

No one would understand. They might not even believe her. It was, after all, an outrageous, implausible story—that God had come to her, and that the baby she carried was to be the Messiah, born of a virgin, a miracle child.

An image of Joseph rose up in her mind, and tears stung her eyes once more. How would he be able to bear this news—that his unspoiled bride, for whom he had waited so long, now held a baby in her womb? Not the son of his seed, but Someone Else. He would be devastated, humiliated. The Law said that he could have her stoned. At the very least, he could walk away and never look back. He could easily find another wife with whom to build a life and bear children.

An invisible sword pierced Mary's heart, and she gasped as the pain wracked her soul. God had spoken, and she had said yes. No matter what the cost, she would not be disobedient in the face of the Almighty. She could not—would not—change her mind. But it was a yes that would alter her life forever.

33

She wept until she had no more tears to cry. She did not know how much time had passed, but when she arose from the mat, the moon had shifted low on the western horizon. A thin sliver of blue light came through the window and bathed her face with its illumination.

Mary ran a hand through her hair, straightened her dress, and lit the candle that sat on the center of the table. Her stomach rumbled, and the scent of the bread she had baked that morning beckoned to her. By candlelight she broke off a corner of the bread and poured a little wine into a cup. With the bread and wine in her hands, she walked to the doorway and gazed out into the night sky.

Thousands of tiny stars blinked back from the velvety blackness that spanned the horizon. She felt so small, so alone, so insignificant. And yet one star—one large, bright, pulsing light—seemed to aim its rays directly toward her, as if sending a message. Perhaps she was not alone, after all.

Mary watched the star for a moment, then dipped the bread into the cup and brought it to her lips. The flavors of wine and bread filled her mouth and comforted her. The bread, sweet and yeasty; the wine, sharp and savory. Like her life, she mused—bittersweet, a merging of joy and pain, blessing and sorrow, faith and fear.

Despite the pain, despite the fear, she knew instinctively that her answer to Gabriel had been the right one. "Let it be to me as you have spoken," she repeated in a whisper. "Whatever the sacrifice, whatever the loss, I am your servant."

sther looked up from sweeping the floor and saw her daughter Mary standing in the doorway. The girl had dark circles under her eyes, but her face looked radiant, as if illuminated by some inner fire.

"How long have you been up, Mother? Why didn't you wake me?"

Esther set the broom in the corner and went over to her daughter. She ran one hand over Mary's dark hair and cupped a palm around her cheek. "I heard you stirring about late last night—very late, I think. Did you have trouble sleeping?"

Mary nodded. "A little."

"Your conscience is bothering you?" Esther raised one eyebrow.

"What—what do you mean?" The girl flushed and looked away.

"Nothing, child. It was just a joke." She pointed toward the hearth, where a pot of porridge bubbled. "Come, have some breakfast."

The light went out of Mary's countenance, and her skin paled. "No, I—I don't feel like eating."

"Are you ill, child?" Esther peered into her daughter's face. Something was wrong, something Mary did not want to talk about. "Sit down," she said, "and tell me what's bothering you."

With obvious reluctance, Mary sat, staring at the table top and fiddling with a lock of hair.

She didn't look up, and every time Esther tried to catch her gaze, she avoided eye contact.

Now Esther was certain that something was amiss. Mary never acted like this. They had always been close, always talked to one another about everything. After her betrothal to Joseph had been announced, the girl had even dared to ask her mother what being a wife was like. They had no secrets, nothing to hide. Until now.

"Mary, is there something you want to talk about?"

The girl nodded, still not meeting Esther's eyes. "I—I have to tell you, but I don't quite know how to explain this. I'm—I'm afraid you won't believe me."

"When have I ever not believed you, child?" Esther snorted. "Have you ever lied to me?"

"No."

"And I don't expect you to lie now. Nor do I expect you to keep something from me that I ought to know. I am your mother, after all. Now what is it?"

Mary took a deep breath, and tears filled her eyes. "Mother, I'm—I'm expecting."

"Expecting what?"

The girl shook her head in obvious frustration. "I am going to have a baby," she said deliberately.

She started to say something else, but Esther didn't hear it. Rage rose up within her—a blinding fury that someone had taken advantage of her child, a white-hot fear of the truth. Then suddenly her mind cleared, and she spat out, "Joseph!" She turned back to Mary. "I knew it was a mistake to promise you to a man so much older than you! I told your father something like this might happen, but would he listen to me? No! He assured me that Joseph was an honorable man, a—"

"Mother!"

Her daughter's voice interrupted the tirade, and Esther sank into the chair opposite Mary. "What?"

"It—it wasn't Joseph."

"Not Joseph? Who, then? Whoever it is, we'll go to the priest! We'll demand justice! The Law will not let a man—any man—take a woman by force and get away with it." She shook her head. "Dear God—do you know what this means? Joseph will reject you; he will have no other choice. He will—"

38

Mary steadied her hands on the table. "Please, Mother, just listen. No one took me by force."

Esther felt her anger crumple into despair. "You *consented?*"

"In a manner of speaking, yes," her daughter whispered. "Now, please, just sit still for a minute and allow me to explain."

Esther stared at Mary. What on earth was there to explain? That her daughter had voluntarily allowed herself to be violated, and now found herself with child when she was engaged to another man? No amount of explaining in the world could make her understand.

But she didn't say so. Instead, she forced herself to be calm. She folded her hands on the table and squeezed them until her knuckles turned white. "All right. I'm listening."

"Last night, after you and Papa went to sleep, I had a visitor—"

"Here? In our own home? I can't believe—"

"Mother, please don't interrupt. Let me finish."

"All right. But if it was just last night, how can you be sure—?"

"I'll explain that, too," Mary cut in. "I'll explain everything, if only you'll give me a chance."

"Go on."

"The visitor was not a *man*, Mother. He was an *angel*. A messenger sent from God."

Esther rolled her eyes, but said nothing.

"He told me that the Lord had sent him to bring me good news—that I would conceive

Don't you understand what this means, Mother? I have been chosen to be the Vessel of the Holy One.

and bear a child, and that the baby would be Messiah, the Anointed One." She stopped and gazed placidly at Esther.

"And you expect me to believe this?" Esther retorted.

"It's true. After he left, a bright light filled the room, and a Presence—I can't find any other way to describe it—came upon me. When it was all over, I knew—don't ask me how, but I knew. There was a child growing in my womb, a baby conceived through a miracle. Don't you understand what this means, Mother? I have been chosen to be the Vessel of the Holy One, the

One our people have waited for all these years. The Savior. The Son of the Most High."

Esther put her head down on the table and sighed. Her hands shook, and she felt as if she were going to be sick. She had tried to tell her husband that it was a mistake, teaching Torah to a girl. An excess of religion could be damaging to a young woman. But he had insisted; his daughter, he said, would be a woman of faith—her own faith, not her husband's or the rabbi's. She would know for herself what it meant to love and serve God, and she would make him proud.

Well, how proud would he be now, when he found out that his precious daughter's religious training had resulted in this? Clearly, the child was demented, concocting a story about an angelic messenger and a baby from God. Perhaps it had been too much for her, the realization that her sin would certainly cost her everything—perhaps even her life.

"You do believe me, don't you, Mother?" The words came as if from a great distance, the voice of a pleading child.

"How can I believe you?" Esther whispered. She looked up into her daughter's face and saw there an expression of total despair. "You said you consented to this?"

"Yes," Mary choked out. "I told the angel, 'Let it be to me as you have said.' And then the Presence came over me in the form of a bright light."

"Your father and I were here, asleep in the next room!" Esther's words came out in a groan. "We saw no light, heard no voice. Nothing except you moving around in the darkness." She groped for an explanation. "Perhaps it was all a dream. It's much too early to know if you are with child or not. Maybe it was just a concoction of your vivid imagination."

"I did not imagine this, Mother. Nor did I dream it." Tears welled up in Mary's eyes and spilled over. "It's the truth. Why don't you trust me? You said yourself I've never lied to you."

Esther shook her head. "Until now. I understand, Mary, why you would want to explain this in a way that makes you look innocent. You'll pay a very high price for your mistake—we all will. But it's blasphemy to blame God for your sin."

She paused, and after a moment or two began to reason through the options open to them. "I think it might be best if you went away for a while. Perhaps your cousin Elizabeth would take you in for a few months—"

Mary's countenance brightened. "Oh, I almost forgot. The angel told me that Elizabeth is expecting a baby, too. She's in her sixth month—another miracle. Don't you understand, Mother? This is all part of a divine plan—"

"A plan?" Esther gritted her teeth. "The only plan I see is that you've made up this story to relieve yourself of responsibility for your actions. But whatever you've done—whether you've deceived yourself into believing this, or are just trying to deceive everyone

41

else—I don't want you to suffer. Yes, going to stay with Elizabeth might be the best thing."

Mary rose from the table and faced her mother squarely. Esther saw in her daughter's eyes a look of determination, even defiance. "All right. I'll go to Elizabeth's. I'll disappear for a while so I won't shame you any further." She closed her eyes for a moment, and a single tear seeped from her eyelid and rolled down her cheek. "But tell me one thing, Mother—why, when our people have been waiting for centuries to see the coming of Messiah, is such a miracle so hard to believe?"

Esther considered the question. "Because you are my daughter," she said at last.

Mary walked to the door and turned to look at her mother one last time. "There's something I need to do," she said. "Then I'll be back to prepare for the journey."

"You're going to tell Joseph?"

"I am." Her daughter nodded decisively. "He may not accept my word, but it's a chance I'll have to take. One way or another, he should hear it from me."

"You're ruining your life, you know," Esther murmured.

"I'm being obedient to God," Mary corrected. Then she was gone.

For a long time Esther sat at the table and tried to sort out the emotions that did battle in her heart. She wanted to trust the daughter she loved so much, but she couldn't bring herself to believe Mary's story. It was too farfetched, too completely outrageous. A miraculous conception, a virgin birth? Maybe such a thing *had* been prophesied, but not in her family. Not for her Mary. It was preposterous.

No one else, she was sure, would ever believe it, either.

oseph found a shadowed corner of the temple and waited while Rabbi Ben-Judah completed his duties. Nazareth was a small town, and he wanted to be as discreet as possible. When Ben-Judah turned and looked in his direction, Joseph motioned him over.

"What is it, my son?" Ben-Judah waddled in Joseph's direction. A short, rotund man with a perpetually flushed complexion surrounded by a gray frizz of hair and beard, the priest reminded Joseph of a very old pig. It was a decidedly unkosher image, and it almost made Joseph smile. Almost, but not quite. At this moment he had very little to smile about— especially given the circumstances that brought him to the Rabbi.

The old man's eyes narrowed, and he peered up into Joseph's face. "You seem troubled, Joseph."

Joseph hesitated, then nodded. "Is there somewhere we could talk? Somewhere . . . private?"

Ben-Judah led him outside, to a small grove of palm trees where several benches were clustered together in the shade. "Sit, my son. We will not be disturbed here."

Joseph sat, propping his elbows on his knees and clenching his hands together. He had no idea how to begin, how to tell the Rabbi what had happened to him, and what was about to happen.

"Joseph?" Ben-Judah prodded.

Joseph let out a ragged sigh. "Yes, Rabbi?"

"You came to talk to me? So, talk."

"I am a carpenter, Rabbi. A simple man with simple dreams. But suddenly my life has become very complex, and I don't know what to do. I don't know how to say what I need to say." He felt a wrenching in his gut, and tears filled his eyes.

"Just speak what is in your heart."

Joseph took a deep breath and nodded. "You know I am engaged to be married."

"Of course. Is that what is bothering you? Nervous, are you, about your upcoming wedding? That's perfectly normal, my boy. Your life will change, certainly, but it will undoubtedly change for the better. Mary is a wonderful girl. We should all be so lucky."

"No," Joseph protested. "It's not that. It's—well, something else." He paused and shook his head. "You must promise to tell no one what I am about to tell you."

"I am a priest, Joseph. Your secrets are safe with me."

"Rabbi, do you believe in angels?"

Ben Judah squinted until his beady little eyes almost disappeared. "Angels?"

"Yes, angels. Messengers from God."

"I would not be a very devout priest if I did not believe. I admit I have never had the privilege of seeing one, but—"

"But I *have* seen one!" Joseph blurted out. "At least, I think I have. A few days ago Mary came to me with some news that confused and frightened me." He steeled himself to say the words. "She is *with child*, Rabbi. And before you ask, no, I have not touched her. And according to her, no other man has, either. The baby, she says, is a gift from God. The Messiah, the Chosen One."

"And you believe her?"

"At first I didn't know what to believe. I was devastated. I saw my entire future crumble to dust before my eyes. But, Rabbi, I knew that no matter what she had done, I still loved her. I did not want to see her shamed and humiliated—and certainly not stoned for adultery. I had determined that I would break the engagement quietly, that she could go away somewhere—"

"Yet I see in your face that your resolve has changed?"

Joseph nodded. "For several nights I didn't sleep at all. I couldn't get it out of my mind. I was angry, and hurt, and then—" He stopped suddenly, unable to go on.

"And where, might I ask, does the angel come into this story?" Ben-Judah prompted.

"I'm getting to that. As I said, I hadn't slept for days. I couldn't work, and I was exhausted. Finally my body couldn't take the strain any longer. I fell asleep. And as I slept, I dreamed that an angel came to me."

45

"And said—?"

"He said that I shouldn't be afraid. That I should go ahead and take Mary as my wife. That she had spoken truly, and the baby she had conceived was from the Holy Spirit. The child would be a son, the angel said, and I was to call his name Jesus, for he would save the people from their sins." Joseph closed his eyes and shook his head. "When I awoke, I felt a sense of peace. But now that peace has vanished, and I'm beginning to wonder if it really happened. Could I have imagined it?"

Ben-Judah did not speak for a moment, then took a deep breath. "You could have imagined it, yes. You are a righteous man, Joseph, a man of great integrity and honor. It could be that deep down, you are looking for a way to justify taking Mary as your wife, even though the child she carries is not yours." He paused, then continued. "On the other hand, your conversation with the angel could be real—as real as the discussion we are having right now." He smiled up into Joseph's face. "I'm not sure it matters one bit whether the angel was real or a product of your imagination."

"How can you say it doesn't matter?" Joseph snapped. "I have always sought to obey the law of Moses; I have no right to ignore it when it doesn't suit me. Only God can set aside the law."

Ben-Judah chuckled. "Perhaps *you* should have been the priest, Joseph."

"I am no priest. That's why I came to you for advice. What must I do?"

"You already know the answer to that question, my son."

Joseph felt his anger flaring. "If I knew the answer," he said through gritted teeth, "we would not be having this discussion at all."

"Of course we would," the Rabbi countered. "You are not seeking advice so much as confirmation. You have already received your answer. You have said, and rightly so, that only God can set aside the law. But whether this word came directly from an angelic messenger or from your own heart makes no difference. The direction you have been given still derives from God. And far be it from me, even as a priest of the temple, to second-guess the Almighty."

The gentle insistence in Ben-Judah's voice worked its way into Joseph's soul. For a fleet-

The gentle insistence in Ben-Judah's voice worked its way into Joseph's soul.

47

ing moment, the Rabbi's voice reminded him of the angel's. The sense of peace he had felt upon awakening from his dream returned, and with it, the assurance that Ben-Judah's words were true. Joseph *did* have his answer.

He exhaled a heavy sigh and felt a weight lift from his shoulders. "Thank you, Rabbi," he murmured.

"Don't thank me," the priest responded. "Thank the Almighty for directing you, before you made a decision you might have regretted for the rest of your life."

Joseph smiled, stood, and stretched the kinks out of his back. "Mary has gone to visit her cousin," he said. "When she returns, we will have a marriage ceremony to prepare for."

"I will anticipate it with great joy." Ben-Judah shook Joseph's hand and clapped him on the shoulder. "Shalom, my friend. Go with God."

Joseph turned to leave, but the Rabbi's voice arrested him. "One more thing—"

He looked over his shoulder. "Yes?"

"Just for the record, I do believe in angels."

Joseph grinned. "So do I, Rabbi."

"Hold onto that faith, my son, and keep your eyes open."

"I will," Joseph promised. And in his heart of hearts, he knew that the next time an answer came—either from God's messenger or from the depths of his own soul—he would be ready.

The Joy

REUNION

lizabeth leaned back into the shade of the canvas awning over the doorway and squinted out into the morning sunlight toward a distant rise. She had always viewed the hills of Judea as a welcome, comforting presence, like strong protective sentinels guarding the village. But today she wished they would move over a bit and give her a better view of the horizon, for Elizabeth was eagerly anticipating the arrival of a visitor.

The last time Elizabeth had seen her, Mary had been little more than a child. Surely she had grown—she was, what? Thirteen? Not a fully matured woman, yet, but still engaged to be married. And now, for what reason Elizabeth did not know, she was making the journey from Nazareth to visit her old cousin.

Such a sweet girl, Mary was. Raised to honor and respect her elders, she treated Elizabeth more like a grandmother than a distant relative. And even though they lived apart and rarely saw each other, Elizabeth's heart had leaped for joy at the news that Mary was coming to see her.

What would the dear girl think, Elizabeth wondered, when she discovered that her old cousin was with child? She hoped that Mary would share her excitement, perhaps even stay with her until the baby was born.

As if he had read her mind, the infant stirred in her womb. A faint kick, then a stronger one, so powerful that it nearly took her breath away. Elizabeth shifted, trying to find a more comfortable position, and then looked up at the horizon again.

There! In the distance—a small donkey made its way down the hillside, stirring up dust along the road, with a diminutive rider on its back. The beast was too far away for Elizabeth to see much detail, but her heart bubbled to life like a spring of water.

Closer, closer—yes! It was Mary! Her dark hair flowed long and loose beneath a blue head covering, and she lifted her hand to wave. At last the donkey came to a stop near the doorway, and the girl dismounted, approaching her cousin with outstretched arms.

"Elizabeth!" Mary called. "It is so good to see you after all this time!"

Elizabeth opened her mouth to respond, but no words came. The babe in her womb gave a mighty leap, and she stood there for a moment, breathless, her mind filled with images she did not understand. Then, just as suddenly, as if the noonday sun had come out from behind a cloud, the truth dawned on her.

"Blessed are you among women, and blessed is the fruit of your womb!" she blurted out. "But who am I, that the mother of my Lord should come to me?" The words startled Elizabeth, as if they had come from some source other than her own mind. Still, she had only to take one glance at Mary's radiant countenance to know that wherever the words came from, she had spoken truly. Mary *was* with child. Elizabeth knew it, even though there were no outward signs. And she knew, just as surely, that the infant in her cousin's womb was the Chosen One.

The young girl stared at her with an expression of wonder and incredulity. "You *know?*"

Elizabeth stepped forward and held Mary in a close embrace. "As soon as I heard the sound of your greeting, the child within my womb danced for joy. Blessed is she who believed that there would be a fulfillment of all the Lord has spoken to her."

Elizabeth listened in awe as Mary sang the praises of the Almighty, and tears filled her eyes.

53

Mary stepped back and raised her arms heavenward. "My soul magnifies the Lord," she whispered, "and my spirit has rejoiced in God my Savior. For the Lord has looked with favor on his humble servant, and from this day forth all generations will call me blessed. The Mighty One has done great things for me, and Holy is his name."

Elizabeth listened in awe as Mary sang the praises of the Almighty, and tears filled her eyes. She had lived long and seen much, and after the conception of her own son, she never dreamed that any other act of God could be quite so grand. But here she was, face to face with the ultimate miracle—the enfleshing of the Holy in the body of her own dear Mary. Messiah had come at last, and Elizabeth herself would be not only mother to the Forerunner, but great-grandmother—in practice, if not in reality—to the Holy One of God.

At last they went inside, where Elizabeth set out fresh bread and fruit and a little goat's milk, and listened while Mary told her story.

"And your mother didn't *believe* you?" Elizabeth fumed. "How could she possibly think that you would—"

"She is my mother," Mary answered placidly. "She wants to protect me, to shield me from getting hurt."

"Well, so would I, my dear. But how can she possibly imagine she's protecting you by accusing you of lying?" Despite her anger, Elizabeth chuckled. "Besides, she must think you a very creative liar, to come up with a story such as this one."

Mary laughed lightly. "It is a kind of compliment, I suppose. But—" her countenance sobered. "Mother—like Joseph, like everyone else—will simply have to draw her own conclusions. She can choose to believe, or not to believe."

"And what of Joseph, that nice young man of yours?" Elizabeth asked cautiously. "What has he chosen?"

"Joseph has chosen to believe," Mary answered. "Although it was not an easy decision for him. He didn't know what to make of my story at first. Initially, he wanted to break our engagement and quietly send me away so I wouldn't be subjected to humiliation. But then something happened. He changed his mind."

"God spoke to him." Elizabeth surprised even herself with the firmness of this opinion. "This child of yours needs a father. A strong father. A noble, godly man like Joseph."

Mary nodded. "I would not have contested any decision he might have made," she said quietly. "But I can't tell you how thankful I am that he still intends to marry me. You're right, Elizabeth. This baby needs him. And I need him, too."

"And God," Elizabeth added in a whisper, "somehow provides all that we need."

Mary slipped into silence, and her eyes took on a faraway expression, as if she were looking into the future. Elizabeth watched as a series of emotions flitted across the girl's face—joy and pain, sorrow and exultation, terror and longing and hope.

This sweet child of her heart, she knew instinctively, would not have an easy life. Her obedience would cost her dearly—she had already begun to get a glimpse of the price she would pay for saying yes to God. But obedience brought great spiritual riches, as well. The knowledge that she had been chosen as an instrument of God's grace, not just for herself, but for all God's people. The awareness that some—not all, but perhaps a great many—*would* believe, and would be blessed because of her.

55

Elizabeth could only pray that in the long run, the joy would be greater than the heartbreak.

FATHERHOOD

oseph bent over his workbench and planed the fragrant cedar plank until it was as smooth as the stones along the riverbank. There could be no jagged edges, no splinters in this wood. It was to become a crib, created by his own work-roughened hands. A baby bed. For his baby. His son.

Joseph missed Mary terribly, but in many ways, these months apart had been a good thing. It had given him time to think, to plan. Time to sand off his own rough edges of emotion. Time to resolve the questions, to discover what was truly in his heart.

What he had discovered, at his deepest core, was love.

Love for Mary, the woman to whom he had pledged himself, heart and soul, mind and strength. Love for the child that grew in her womb. Love for the life they would build together.

It would have been easy for him to submit out of a sense of duty—to marry her in order to shield her from scandal and disgrace, and to protect himself from the shame and dishonor of breaking the vows he had made to God and to his beloved. He had acquiesced to the angel's command, but half-expected to resent his compliance, to feel trapped, unwillingly resigned to a situation over which he had no control.

Now, miraculously, everything had changed. Once the obedience was accomplished, once he had chosen to believe Mary's story and respond to the angel's direction, another emotion took hold. Not resentment, but acceptance. Not resignation, but liberation.

Rather than being trapped, Joseph found himself free. Free to love Mary more than he had ever loved her before. Free to marry her, and equally free to resist his desire for her and

Joseph hadn't realized at first that this was the answer to all his prayers and dreams and hopes for his life.

not touch her until after the child was born. Free, most importantly, to love and care for that baby as his own.

And the boy *was*, in Joseph's mind, his son. Not the offspring of his body, of course, but the son of his heart, the child of his soul. In pensive moments, Joseph thought of the unborn infant as *Jesus Ben-Joseph*, and the idea caused him to swell with pride. The pride of a father for his firstborn. The pride of a man whose life has been fulfilled in a family of his own.

A smile tugged at the corners of Joseph's mouth. They would have a good life, he and Mary and Jesus—and whatever sons and daughters might come after. A life filled with simple pleasures and uncomplicated joys.

In his confusion and despair over Mary's announcement, Joseph hadn't realized at first that this was the answer to all his prayers and dreams and hopes for his life. Not exactly in the form he had expected, he had to admit, but he could not—would not—deny the truth. God, after all, often answered prayers in unanticipated ways. This, he now understood, was the answer to his unspoken longing for meaning and significance in life.

For what could be more significant than becoming a father? What was more important than the opportunity to direct the life of a child, to train him in the ways of the Almighty, to help him grow toward the fulfillment of his own destiny?

And this child, he knew, had an important destiny to fulfill.

Joseph wasn't exactly certain what it all meant—that the infant in Mary's womb was the Chosen One, the long-awaited Messiah. If you gathered a dozen Jews together, you would have a dozen opinions of what kind of mission the Messiah would have. Some thought he would stand as a mighty warrior and do battle against the great armies of Rome. Some believed he would rise up as a political leader to challenge oppression; others looked for a prophet, a teacher, the greatest Rabbi Israel had ever known. A few held to the belief that he would give himself to the downtrodden—feeding the hungry, healing the sick, working miracles to demonstrate his origins in God. But all held one opinion in common—that when he came, the whole world would see, and know, and believe.

Joseph wasn't so sure. He had begun to wonder if the Almighty might not have something else in mind, altogether. Some kind of mission that might depend in part upon his own influence, and Mary's, in what kind of person this child would turn out to be.

Joseph looked down at his hands—large, powerful hands, padded with calluses; arms ridged with taut, lean muscles. He inhaled the fresh scent of the wood, and his eyes drifted to the frame, already completed, for the baby's crib. It would be a fine piece of work—carved at head and foot, with a gentle curve underneath so that Mary could rock the child to sleep. Padded and lined with sheepskin, bleached white in the Judean sun. His masterpiece of carpentry, designed to soothe and comfort the tiny Masterpiece of creation.

Joseph loved being a carpenter—a builder of things designed to endure. Stout tables and rugged chairs. Milking stools and plows and yokes for the gentle oxen. Water troughs and mangers, wooden trenchers to carry fresh-baked bread and ripened fruit. Doors to hold in the warmth of a fire, and gates to keep wolves out of sheepfolds.

All these skills, and more, he would pass on to his son.

Joseph could imagine the two of them, standing together at this very bench, as he taught those tender hands how to use the adze and miter and plane. In his mind's eye he saw the dark curly head bending intently over a plank, little brown feet planted firmly on the ground in an attitude of determination. He could envision the boy growing into a man, tall and strong, with sensitive, compassionate eyes and shoulders broad enough to carry the weight of the world. He could see those massive arms stretched out to measure the length of a beam, could even, if he tuned his ear to listen into the future, hear the echo of hammer striking nails.

It was a profound calling, fatherhood. An occupation that demanded a lifetime of commitment, a job that humbled and awed him and presented him with the greatest challenge he would ever face. But the more he thought about it, the more he realized that it was a vocation he had waited for all his life.

Joseph fitted the cedar plank in place and nailed it to the bottom of the crib, then stepped back to survey his handiwork. It was a fine crib, sturdy and strong and marked by the touch of a master's hand. A bed worthy of a carpenter's son, destined to follow in his father's footsteps and be about his father's business.

"I will teach you everything I know, my son," he murmured, "and you will make me proud."

Joseph smiled to himself and stroked the satiny wood with a gentle touch. Yes, his son would grow up to be like him—a man who understood the importance of building something that lasts. A man whose life could be measured by the strength of a beam rising to the sky, and the power of nails holding the universe in place.

hem set up his table in the market square and laid out the tools of his trade: a carved wooden box for the tax money he would gather over the next few weeks, pens and ink and paper for the census Emperor Augustus had decreed, and a second, smaller box for his portion of the proceeds.

At the moment the square was quiet—a couple of women at the well, drawing their morning water and gossiping; two or three tradesmen setting up their wares for the day. By noon, however, the sleepy little village of Bethlehem would be crowded to capacity by travelers wanting to get registered, pay their taxes, and get on with their lives.

A lot of people stood to make a great deal of money in the coming weeks. The proprietor of Bethlehem's single small inn wore a smile so broad it threatened to stretch his face out of shape. He had never seen anything like it. Already the inn was booked nearly to capacity. Anyone who looked poor and ragged he turned away—he could get premium prices from the wealthier visitors who didn't know, or didn't care, what his usual rates were.

Shem had booked a room for himself and his ten-year-old son, who was traveling with him. The boy already showed signs of becoming quite the financial prodigy. He understood the principles of tax collecting better than most adults, and would no doubt join his father's business when he was grown. He had watched with quiet respect as Shem managed to bargain the innkeeper down with the assurance that he would be staying for several weeks, and the implication that the innkeeper's own taxes might be reduced if he gave the tax collector a break.

When the deal had been sealed, the boy questioned his father about his promise. Shem explained, much to the lad's amusement, that he had no intention of cutting his profits. Taxation was a lucrative venture, an enterprise that allowed no room for personal feelings or empty promises. Rome got its share, and whatever else Shem could extort from the citizens was his to keep. It was true enough that tax collectors were despised, but if you had enough money, you didn't need respect. In this business, as in so many others, greed was the trait that kept you alive.

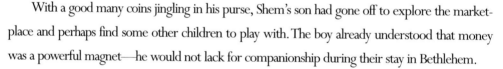

With a good many coins jingling in his purse, Shem's son had gone off to explore the market-place and perhaps find some other children to play with. The boy already understood that money was a powerful magnet—he would not lack for companionship during their stay in Bethlehem.

By afternoon, just as Shem had predicted, the lines had grown long and almost every-one was irritable and out of sorts. No one liked paying taxes, especially when they knew they were being assessed unfairly. He had already had a few shouting matches with irate citizens, but in the end the fear of Rome's power made them pay. By the time dusk fell, the crowds were beginning to thin out a little—travelers caught by the darkness would simply camp outside the village and come in to register the next morning.

Shem was just about to close up for the night when he saw a couple coming his way—a tall, broad-shouldered fellow accompanied by a young girl riding a small gray donkey.

They moved slowly, and as they approached, Shem could see that they were exhausted. They had probably traveled for days, and from the looks of her, the woman was nearly ready to deliver a baby.

Worse luck for him. If the child had already been born, Shem could have imposed a tax upon it, too. The father would have to pay for three instead of two. Why couldn't they have waited another day or two? He could make them wait, of course—could just tell them to come back tomorrow. Perhaps by then the baby would arrive. But Shem's experience had taught him, too, that weary people were less likely to contest their tax rate. If they were tired or hungry or in a hurry, they simply paid up without giving him an argument.

"Shalom," the man said in a quiet voice. "Are we too late to register?"

The tone in the man's voice, as well as his words, shook Shem to the core. No one ever offered peace to a tax collector. And few spoke in such a considerate manner.

He squinted in the gathering gloom at the two who stood before him. A laboring man, judging from his rough clothes and the calluses on his hands. A vineyard worker, perhaps. His gaze shifted to the expectant wife. She was little more than a child herself, with wide brown eyes and an innocent expression. Something about her tugged at his heart, but he couldn't identify the feeling. Was it . . . compassion?

No, he reminded himself sternly. *It's late, and you're hungry, but don't let yourself be taken in by these two.* They would pay just like everyone else, no matter how pathetic they looked.

"I am Joseph of Nazareth, in Galilee," the man said in that same quiet voice. "From the house of David. This is my wife, Mary." The man gazed at the girl with an expression of deep love, and gently helped her down from the donkey's back. "We've come to register, according to the Emperor's decree, and to pay the tax we owe to Rome." He withdrew a small leather pouch from a bag at his waist. "I hope we have enough."

Shem fought against the temptation to take pity on this couple, so far from home and

The young boy stared into her eyes, mesmerized. "You're so beautiful," he whispered in an awestruck voice.

with so few resources at their disposal. But before he could say anything, the man named Joseph smiled. "And who is this handsome young fellow?"

Shem turned to see his son standing beside him, his eyes round and wide as he surveyed the ragged-looking couple. "My son," Shem explained. He watched as the boy approached the young girl and reached out as if to grasp her hand.

"I'm Zacchaeus. What's your name?"

"I'm Joseph," the man chuckled. "And my wife, Mary." He grinned down at the lad.

The young boy stared into her eyes, mesmerized. "You're so beautiful," he whispered in an awestruck voice. "Are you going to have a baby?"

"I am," Mary answered quietly. "Very soon. And I hope he'll be as handsome and as courteous as you are."

"Let the people get on with their business, Zacchaeus," Shem prompted. "I'm sure they must be weary from their travels and eager to find a place to stay."

"Indeed we are," Joseph answered. "It's been a difficult journey, especially for Mary, in her condition."

"We're staying at the inn," Zacchaeus blurted out. "They might have another room for you, or if you don't have enough money, you could stay with us, in our room—"

"Now, son, I'm sure they wouldn't want to do that," Shem corrected. "They will find their own place."

"But, Papa—"

"Excuse us for a moment, please." Shem drew his son aside. "What do you think you're doing?"

"I was just—just trying to help," Zacchaeus stammered. "It's obvious, Papa, that they don't have very much money, and she's going to have a baby, and even if the inn is full, we've got plenty of room, and—"

"How many times have I told you?" Shem interrupted. "You don't get anywhere in this business by caring about people. You don't look at the faces. You take the names, collect the money, and keep your mind on your job."

"Yes, Papa, but—"

"No buts. Not another word, now." He went back to his table, where Mary and Joseph still stood, waiting patiently.

"Don't worry," Joseph said. "We have no intention of imposing upon you. But we do appreciate your son's offer. He's a very kind and compassionate boy."

Traits I will have to work out of him as quickly as possible, Shem thought to himself. To Joseph, he said, "Let's get this finished, shall we?" He consulted his ledger, quoted an amount, and watched while the man counted out his coins.

"Papa!" Zacchaeus tugged on his tunic.

Shem bent down to his son. "What?"

"You only charged him what he owed the Emperor. You didn't take any for yourself."

"Keep quiet. I'll explain later."

But Shem wasn't at all certain that he *could* explain it—to his son, or even to himself. Something had come over him—a brief flash of remorse, perhaps, or sympathy. Maybe even a moment of humanity. He had fully intended to take his share and more, if possible. But when Joseph reached into his bag and retrieved his pitiful collection of coins, Shem simply couldn't bring himself to do it. There was something in the man's demeanor that stopped him. Something in the young girl's eyes that kept him from doing what he had been doing all his adult life. When he looked at them, he felt a touch of . . . of *grace*, he thought. And for just a moment, another emotion he rarely experienced: *shame*.

"Thank you," Joseph said when the transaction was done. "Blessings upon you, and upon your son." He tousled the boy's head and smiled, and they started off.

When they were gone, Zacchaeus frowned up at Shem. "Why did you do it, Papa? Why didn't you take your profit from their taxes?"

Shem shook his head. "I can't explain it, son. There was something about them. Something special." He gave Zacchaeus a stern look. "But it's not a practice I'll make a habit of, you understand."

"I understand, Papa. I know how tax collecting works. But still, I'm glad you did it." He fixed his father with a wistful expression. "Will they be in Bethlehem long?"

"I have no idea. Why do you ask?"

"I liked them," Zacchaeus responded. "And I wanted to see their baby when it's born. Do you think I might be able to?"

Shem gathered up his papers and money boxes, and together they headed for the inn. "I doubt it," he said. In his heart of hearts, Shem fervently hoped that his son would never meet up with this couple and their child again. He wanted Zacchaeus to grow up like him— tough and independent and able to take care of himself. He didn't want his son changed by the influence of the likes of Mary and Joseph and their unborn child.

But he didn't say so. Instead, he said, "Who knows? Maybe you will run across them again. You'll just have to keep your eyes open, I suppose."

"I'll do that, Papa," the boy answered. "I'll watch and wait and hope. And maybe some- day I'll find them again and get to see their baby."

Shem looked down into his son's eager face, and a flash of dread coursed through him. Something in his gut told him that his boy *would* meet up with them again—when or where or how, Shem did not know. But the result, he feared, might change Zacchaeus's life forever.

69

iriam, come and look at these numbers! You won't believe it!"

"I'm busy, Joab. This lamb won't cook itself, you know."

"It can wait for two minutes, can't it? You must see this!"

With an exasperated sigh, Miriam left the fire and went over to the corner of the room, where her husband sat poring over his ledgers. The man could be impossible at times. The inn was crowded almost to capacity, and soon the guests would be demanding their dinner. But no, Joab had to have her attention *right now*, whether their lodgers got fed or not. He had no idea how much work she did around here—cooking and cleaning and getting rooms ready, making sure there was sufficient food and drink for everyone. The man thought *he* ran the place, just because his name was on the door. But he rarely gave a thought to what he would do without her.

"All right, Joab, I'm here." She peered over his shoulder. "What am I looking at?"

"You, my dear," he said with a dramatic flourish, "are looking at more income in two weeks than we've had in the past two years combined." He grinned at her, and his double chin took on an additional fold. "Perhaps I should send a message to the Emperor, thanking him for organizing this census."

"The people who have traveled for weeks to get to the cities of their ancestors wouldn't thank him," Miriam muttered. "It's a terrible inconvenience for everyone."

"Inconvenience? It's a miracle! It's money in our pockets, Miriam—more money than we ever dreamed of! We can expand, add on more rooms, maybe even open a second inn—"

She stared at the round bald spot on the top of his broad head. "Joab, when these travelers have gone home, everything will go back to being exactly like it was. A few guests here and there, but barely enough to make ends meet. We're in Bethlehem, not Jerusalem, remember?"

He sighed. "I suppose you're right. But let's enjoy it while we have it, shall we?"

Miriam's eyes focused on the numbers in the ledger. "How much are you charging these people, Joab? That looks like twice, or three times our usual rate."

"I'm charging what the market will bear." He turned and raised an eyebrow at her. "Apparently a lot of wealthy people trace their roots to Bethlehem. They're paying what I'm asking. All except for that tax collector and his son." He grinned. "I gave him a lower rate, and in return, he will give me a smaller tax bill. So be nice to him. One hand washes the other, you know."

Miriam opened her mouth to contest her husband's unethical business practices, but a knock on the door arrested her attention. "I'll go."

"No, let me." Joab heaved himself up and lumbered across the common room, an expression of unfettered greed filling his eyes. "We only have a couple of rooms left. They'll be in great demand."

Miriam followed and watched over his shoulder as he opened the door to reveal a young couple—a tall, bearded man and a diminutive, wide-eyed girl obviously in the final stages of pregnancy. Her gaze went first to the girl's swelling midsection, and then to her face, which bore the signs of exhaustion and not a little fear.

"Shalom," the man said in a subdued voice. "Peace be unto this house, and to all who dwell within it."

"And peace to you," Joab responded.

"My wife and I need a place to stay for the night. Perhaps for several nights. We'd like to rent a room."

Joab shook his head. "I'm sorry, my friends, but the inn is full."

"We haven't a great deal of money," the man offered, "but our taxes were not as high as we anticipated. I'm sure it will be enough—"

"As I said, we have no more space." Joab started to shut the door. "Sorry."

Miriam pushed forward and addressed the young couple. "Please, wait there for a moment." She grabbed her husband by the sleeve and jerked him back into the common room. "What do you think you're doing?" she hissed under her breath. "We do have two small rooms still available."

"Did you look at them?" Joab demanded.

"I did. They seem like nice, normal people. And she's with child. We can't turn them away."

"They seem like *paupers*," Joab countered. "They could barely pay the minimum. Then what do we say when someone else comes along—someone rich enough to pay double or triple? Do you expect me to give up a premium price to provide lodging for those two?"

"I expect you to have a heart," Miriam answered. "She could deliver that baby at any minute. Are you really going to leave them out in the cold and let her drop that child like one of our cows—out in the fields, or in the stable?"

"One more reason not to rent to them," Joab added triumphantly. "You want her giving birth here, in our inn? All that mess? Not to mention the noise of a squalling infant disturbing our other guests."

Tears filled her eyes as she looked at the girl's face. "I thought we might have something for you, but apparently I was wrong."

Miriam shook her head. "You can't deny them lodging, Joab, not when we have it to give. It's inhuman—unthinkable."

"It's business. And need I remind you that I make the decisions around here? The answer is no!"

Miriam knew better than to cross her husband when he was in such a mood. But she couldn't live with herself if that young girl or her baby died from exposure. She jerked the door open to find the man and his wife still standing on the doorstep, shivering in the night wind.

"Please forgive the delay," she choked out. Tears filled her eyes as she looked at the girl's face. "I thought we might have something for you, but apparently I was wrong."

"Thank you anyway," the man said with a sigh. "Is there anywhere else we might look?"

"I'm afraid there are no other inns in Bethlehem," Miriam answered.

The young girl tugged at her husband's sleeve. "Joseph, what are we going to do?"

"Shhh, Mary," he soothed. "We'll be all right. We'll find an alleyway, somewhere shielded from the wind—" He turned to face Miriam again. "Forgive us for disturbing you. We'll be on our way now. May God's peace rest upon you." He placed a gentle hand upon his wife's arm and guided her toward the street.

Miriam turned and glared viciously at Joab, who still stood behind her, then wheeled back to the doorway. "Wait!"

The man called Joseph stopped and looked over his shoulder.

"There's a small cave out back, cut into the rock—a stable where we keep the animals. It's not much, but—"

Joseph advanced a few steps toward the door and cocked his head. "How much would you charge?"

Joab leaned forward and was just about to quote a price, but Miriam silenced him with a glance. "No charge. Just a minute—I'll get you a blanket."

"We have blankets," Joseph said. "And the stable will be just fine. Thank you for your generosity—and God bless you."

Miriam pointed to the left. "You'll see a path, behind the inn. It leads directly to the stable."

"We'll find it." Joseph lifted his hand in a wave, and he and the girl and their donkey disappeared into the shadows.

Miriam slept little that night. She could not rid her mind of the piteous image of that forlorn and terrified woman-child as she vanished into the darkness along the path to the stable. Joab had been right, of course—and he missed no opportunity to remind her that he had told her so. Shortly after Joseph and Mary had left, two other patrons came seeking shelter—wealthy patrons, who paid the obscene rate Joab quoted them without question. The inn was full. The coffers were swelling. But Miriam's heart was strangely empty.

Late into the night, long after the moon had set, Miriam still paced the floor listening to her husband's snoring. She went to the window, gazed down in the direction of the stable, and prayed that God would forgive her for conceding to Joab's demands and turning that poor couple away.

As if in answer, she heard something—a reedy cry, like the bawling of a tiny infant. An odd light illuminated the roof of the stable entrance. But where did it come from? The moon had already set, and the area behind the inn was usually dark as pitch.

Miriam turned away from the window and climbed back into bed beside her husband. Surely she had imagined the light, and the sound must have been the calling of a night bird.

Still, she didn't feel quite so empty any more. And as she drifted off to sleep, she thought she heard an echo of Joseph's deep and tranquil voice: "Peace be unto this house, and to all who dwell within it."

ary held tight to Joseph's arm as they made their way down the rocky path toward the stable the innkeeper's wife had offered them. When they reached the doorway, Joseph went inside and lit a lamp, and she followed him in.

The stable was little more than a cave dug out of the rock, with a rough-hewn wooden door, a thatched roof over the entrance, and a few stalls. A mild-mannered cow chewed her cud and watched them from one corner, her udder distended with milk and her half-grown calf at her side. A few sheep milled about in one of the pens. Their own faithful donkey found an empty stall with a manger full of hay and began helping himself to dinner.

Joseph forked some clean hay into a mound, spread the blankets over it, and steadied Mary while she settled herself on the makeshift bed. "I'm sorry," he said.

She looked up into his eyes, which held an expression of profound misery. "Sorry for what?"

"For these . . . accommodations." He shook his head and gestured at their surroundings. "I should be able to do better for you—and for the baby—than this."

"This is fine, Joseph. Much better than being out in the open, or in some dark alley, for the night." She leaned back and let out an exhausted sigh. "I rather like the smell of a barn. The hay, the animals. There's a richness to it, an earthiness."

"At least we'll keep warm." He rummaged in their pack and brought out bread and cheese and a few figs. "And we won't starve. We've even got—" he pointed toward the cow— "fresh milk!"

"Do you think it would be all right? I'd love some milk, but wouldn't it be stealing?"

"It would be an act of mercy," Joseph said with a smile. "Looks to me as if the poor old girl might explode any minute." He went over to the cow's stall, gently moved the calf out of the way, and set the milking stool and bucket into place. "Easy, now," he crooned, stroking the cow on her side. He rubbed his hands to warm them.

The cow made no protest, and Joseph began to relieve her of her burden. Mary could see his broad back bent until his head touched the cow's flanks, could hear the odd rattling sound as the milk hit the bottom of the bucket. The beast let out a low moo of contentment.

Mary lay back against the mound of hay and closed her eyes. It had been a long and difficult journey, and her whole body ached. Joseph had been wonderful—always solicitous, ever trying to ease her discomfort. He couldn't help the fact that the inn had no room for them, and at least God had provided some measure of shelter in their time of need. She just hoped that they would be able to make it back to Nazareth before—

A ragged pain shot through her abdomen, and she cried out.

"Mary? Are you all right."

"I'm fine," she managed. "Just a kick—a hard one."

But it wasn't a kick, and even as inexperienced as Mary was concerning childbirth, she knew the difference instinctively. A second pain came, stronger this time, and she felt a flood of warmth flow out from between her legs. A puddle formed on the blanket beneath her and quickly absorbed into the wool.

"Joseph—"

"I'm almost done. You'll have a nice cup of warm milk in just a minute."

"Forget the milk, Joseph. It's time."

He came around the corner of the stall, bucket in hand. "Time for what?"

Mary gripped her stomach. "Time for the baby. Now!"

Joseph dropped the bucket and ran to her. "Now?"

"Now. At least it's starting now. Mother says that first babies usually take a long time to come. But this seems to be happening awfully quickly—"

"Do you want me to get someone? The innkeeper's wife?"

"No, don't leave me!" She grabbed his hand and held on for dear life.

"All right, I won't leave. But I've never done this before, and—"

Mary clenched her teeth against the contractions. Men could be so exasperating. Of course he had never done this—neither had she. But it was a natural process, she reminded herself, part of God's design. She had seen a birth once, when she attended her mother at a midwifing. Women did this every day and produced healthy, happy babies. And everyone said that after it was all over, you didn't remember the pain for the joy of the birth.

She wondered briefly if they were lying.

She did not, however, have time to give it much thought. Another contraction gripped her, stronger than ever, and she gasped.

"What do I do?"

Mary looked up to see an expression of abject terror on Joseph's face, a panic that mir-rored the fear in her own heart. She took a deep breath and tried to compose herself. God, after all, had done this. God would see them through it.

"I'll be fine," she told him with more confidence than she felt. "Just get that light blanket out of the donkey's pack, and stay close."

Mary looked up to see an expression of abject terror on Joseph's face, a panic that mirrored the fear in her own heart.

In the next few hours, Mary experienced a tumult of emotion unlike anything she had ever imagined. She was afraid, certainly, but she also felt a surge of awe and wonder at the miracle that was taking place. And for a brief moment, she even grappled with a measure of shame. No man, after all, had ever seen her naked; no man had ever touched her. And now her dear Joseph was about to be initiated into the mysteries of womanhood in a most unorthodox way. He almost seemed more embarrassed than she was, but to his credit, he gathered all his reserves of courage and attended to her with grace and compassion.

At last, when she was certain she could stand the pain no longer, she bore down hard, so hard that it felt like a sword piercing her innermost soul.

"I see him!" Joseph shouted. "I can see the crown of his head! He has hair, Mary! Dark hair!" He began to laugh, and Mary reached down and grabbed him by the tunic.

"Pay attention!" she demanded through gritted teeth.

"All right, all right." He looked up at her, and she could see huge tears welling up in his eyes. "Come on, push. You're almost there!"

Mary pushed. Hard. It felt as if she were ripping wide open, and then Joseph cried out, "Here he comes!" With one final monumental effort, the baby slid out into the world.

"Turn him upside down," Mary told him. "And swat him on the bottom."

"How do you know that?"

"I helped my mother at a birthing once. It clears his chest and gets him breathing."

Joseph did as he was instructed, and the slippery infant let out a strangled cry and began yowling at the top of his lungs. "Did I hurt him?"

Mary reached for the baby and laid him across her chest. "No, he's fine. Just a little angry, that's all." She took up the edge of her robe and wiped his face, then cuddled him to her breast.

"He's beautiful," Joseph breathed.

"Not yet, but he will be. Could you hand me something to clean him up with?"

Joseph fumbled for the pack and drew out a clean cloth. "Will this do?"

"Perfect. Also a knife and a bit of string." Mary sank back across the bed of hay. She had never felt so depleted in her life, and yet never so alive. She explained to Joseph how to cut the

81

umbilical cord and tie it off, and when that job was finished, she lay down and let the baby nurse.

"Little Jesus," she crooned, letting her tears fall on the top of his downy head. "Was there ever such a wonder in the world?"

It was, Mary knew, a true miracle, a unique demonstration of the power and glory of God. Her child's conception, his birth, the life he was destined to lead—there were still so many unknowns. But she believed with all her heart that God would continue to guide and direct them.

A miracle, yes. And yet, somehow, it was all so human, too. In a cave, surrounded by animals, without a proper place for the child to lay his head. Bloody and a little barbaric, the way women had been giving birth since the beginning of time.

Joseph lay down beside her and cradled her head on his arm. He reached out one finger and stroked the baby's cheek. "This is the way God chooses to come into the world?" he mused. "In a helpless infant, in a stable, in the darkness?"

Mary's eyes grew heavy, and she snuggled against Joseph's shoulder. "I don't understand it all either, my love," she murmured. "Perhaps we never will. But look at him. What a gift he is."

She drifted toward sleep, and felt a tiny hand clasp around her finger. She might have given life to him, she thought, but he had given life to her as well.

arai turned over on the sleeping mat she shared with her husband Lemuel. The inn was full, and through the wall at her head she could hear the sound of someone snoring. If only she could sleep as soundly!

But Sarai hadn't slept more than two or three hours a night for the past four years. Every time she closed her eyes, she saw the terrible vision of her daughter, her precious Naomi, lying crushed to death under that load of bricks.

It had been a freak accident, everyone said. The oxen pulling the load had shied when a cat skittered across the marketplace in front of them, and the brick cart had overturned just as Naomi was crossing the street. Sarai had seen it all, as if in slow motion—the oxen jerking against their yoke, the cart twisting, the little girl looking up in horror as the bricks smashed into her skull and buried her, with only one thin arm sticking out as if reaching toward her mother. She had watched it happen, and had been helpless to stop it.

Naomi had been Sarai's miracle child. After years of longing for a baby, after losing three before they were ever born, Sarai's prayers had finally been answered. A robust infant girl, with pink cheeks and laughing brown eyes and a head full of thick black hair

Lemuel had tried to hide his disappointment that Sarai had not borne him a son. But he got over it soon enough—no one could resist Naomi's charms, least of all her own father. He bounced her on his knee, carried her everywhere on his shoulders. And when he looked at his daughter, no amount of effort could hide his love for his baby girl. He adored her, and she him.

Lemuel did not exactly blame Sarai for Naomi's death. He knew it wasn't her fault, that no one—not even Lemuel himself—could have prevented it. But after they buried Naomi and observed Shiva for her, things were never quite the same between Sarai and her husband. Once their grief subsided, they carried on life as usual, but they rarely spoke about anything other than the weather or the crops or the need to buy a new cow—and never, never about the daughter they had both loved and lost.

Naomi would have been twelve this year—nearly as old as the one who had come to the inn earlier this evening with her husband by her side. Sarai had watched from her upstairs window as the innkeeper's wife had sent them down to the stable for the night, and her heart had gone out to that girl—barely more than a child herself—who was obviously about to deliver a baby. She had even considered going down to the barn to offer her help to the young couple, but she wasn't sure she could bear the pain of gazing into the girl's face and seeing what her own Naomi might look like, had she lived. And she was very certain she could not hold a newborn in her arms without breaking down completely.

Tears lodged in Sarai's throat. She got up and went to the window once more. Their room looked down into the market square, now dark and deserted. She stood there, gazing out, and wondering for the millionth time what she had done that so displeased the Almighty. She had to have done something wrong; otherwise God would never have taken her child.

Four years she had spent in confession and self-examination. Four fruitless years. And she had come up with nothing—no explanation, no sin, no reason at all that this terrible thing should have happened. Naomi, the miracle, had simply been snatched away.

Sarai felt a movement at her side and looked around. Lemuel was standing there, his eyes fixed on the marketplace, a vacant, pained expression on his face. Was he reliving it too, seeing the crumpled, lifeless form of their only child dead in the town square? He did not touch her—he rarely did these days—but simply stood there, his ragged breathing filling the small rented room.

Together they stood and watched. And then, without warning, a light filled the courtyard below them, illuminating the well, the cobblestoned street, their own faces. Sarai looked at her husband, and saw his eyes lifting to the source of the light—a bright, bright star in the cold black sky. He opened the window, letting in a rush of frigid air, and took a deep breath.

"What did I do wrong, Sarai?" he muttered.

She turned and stared at him. "What did you say?"

Tears filled his eyes and glinted in the light of the star. "I must have done something wrong, that she should die like that. I must have displeased God. But I loved her so much, so very much . . ."

He couldn't go on. His tears overwhelmed him, and he began to sob. Sarai turned and took him in her arms, and he wept like a terrified child.

"Shhh, my darling," she crooned. "It's all right." She groped for words that would comfort him. "It was an accident, Lemuel. A terrible accident. Nothing you or I or anyone could have prevented. No one is responsible—not even God. We have to let her go." The words surprised her even as she spoke them, but she knew in the depths of her heart that what she said was the truth. An important truth. A profound truth, for both of them. Perhaps now she could finally stop blaming herself, stop looking for phantom sins to confess. And maybe, at long last, she could abandon her anger at the Almighty, too.

The light had grown brighter, and Sarai looked up into her husband's face. As she gazed at him, she saw the look of misery give way to something else. Peace. He swiped at his tears and forced a smile.

"Are you cold?"

Sarai shivered. "A little."

88

He reached for the window, intending to close it, but a distant sound arrested his attention. A cry. The wailing of an infant, coming from behind the inn.

Sarai smiled. "It seems that young girl has delivered her child. I pray both of them are all right."

Lemuel put his arms around her and drew her into his warmth. She closed her eyes and relaxed into him, relishing the embrace. It had been so long, so long . . .

"It almost seems," Lemuel mused, "that this bright star announces that child's birth. I wonder who he—or she—is."

"Perhaps it doesn't matter," Sarai whispered, snuggling closer to him. "Perhaps it is enough that any child is born tonight. I thought I would feel envious of that young mother and her new babe. But I don't. What I feel is—"

"Hope?" Lemuel supplied.

"Yes, hope," Sarai agreed. "And maybe—" she paused, unable to speak the words aloud.

"Maybe there is still hope for us?" he finished. "Another child, perhaps?" He smiled down at her, and Sarai saw an expression she thought was gone forever. Love.

"Is it possible?" she asked, trying to stem the anticipation that rose in her breast.

"I don't see why not." He leaned down and planted a kiss on the top of her head.

She didn't know who it was, this infant who arrived at midnight on the beam of the most brilliant star in heaven.

"No child, of course, will ever take the place of our Naomi." Sarai ventured.

"Of course not. We wouldn't expect that. But life must go on."

The distant cry of the newborn infant floated to them on the night breeze, and Sarai laughed. "Apparently life *does* go on, with us or without us."

"Then maybe it's time for us to rejoin the living." Lemuel reached over and closed the window, then took Sarai's hand. "Come back to bed, my wife. We have some talking to do."

Sarai nodded, and followed him to the sleeping mat. She lay down and sighed as his arms went around her, then turned her head and let her eyes linger once more on the bright angle of starlight that filtered in through the window.

She didn't know who it was, this infant who arrived at midnight on the beam of the most brilliant star in heaven. Perhaps it was nobody, just a poor baby born in a stable to homeless and destitute parents. But its cry, and its star, had somehow brought her and Lemuel peace, and hope for tomorrow.

And as she turned back to her husband, she prayed a silent blessing upon the nameless child who had worked such a miracle.

The Plan

onathan!" Benjamin shouted. "You've got a stray!"

Jonathan looked in the direction Benjamin was pointing, and saw a full-bellied ewe just disappearing over the crest of the hill. He swore under his breath. *By all that's holy*, he thought, *why did the Almighty make these animals so infernally stupid?* He motioned to Benjamin and Seth to look after the rest of his flock, then took off after the wandering sheep.

She was the best ewe in his flock, and Jonathan couldn't afford to lose her. But she was an infuriating beast, always going her own way and paying very little mind either to him or to the direction the rest of the sheep were headed. No doubt she would choose tonight, of all nights, to find some thorny thicket and deliver her lamb in a place where he couldn't get to either of them.

Jonathan followed her, calling to her with no result, and trying desperately to keep an eye on her broad backside as she traipsed down the hill. The moon had set, and it was tough going. He could barely make her out in the darkness.

Jonathan loved his job—loved the sheep, most of the time, and loved the freedom of the shepherd's life. He and Seth and Benjamin had worked together for years, finding the best pasture land for grazing, keeping an eye out for wolves and other predators, sitting around the fire at night swapping stories and becoming fast friends.

To tell the truth, Seth and Benjamin were the only friends Jonathan could claim. Shepherds weren't the most popular people in the world—they lived an isolated existence, and the townspeople avoided them whenever possible. Maybe others were put off by the smell of sweat and dung and wet wool that trailed in their wake. Or maybe they were envious of a shepherd's liberty. Whatever the cause, the three of them—and all shepherds—were outcasts in polite society.

Most of the time Jonathan didn't care. Occasionally, when he had to be among others unlike himself, the snubbing stung a bit. But for the most part, he just lived his life as he pleased, enjoyed what he had, and didn't dwell on what he was missing.

He came over a second rise and saw his ewe a stone's throw away, standing on the lip of a deep ravine. He approached cautiously, quietly. If he spooked her, she might go right over the edge of the precipice. But she didn't pay him any mind. She just stood there, gazing up into the heavens, as if something vitally important to a sheep was going on in the night sky.

Jonathan stopped dead in his tracks when he saw what it was. There, far over a distant hill, a star was rising. A shepherd knows the stars, and he was certain he had never seen this one before. It was the biggest, brightest star he had ever encountered. And it wasn't rising gradually, imperceptibly, the way the moon did, but accelerating so fast that he could actually *see* its movement. It couldn't be a comet; it was not arcing across the sky, but going straight *up*, as if pulled by an invisible hand. And its pulsing light was as bright as any moon he had ever seen.

"Seth! Benjamin!" he yelled over his shoulder. "Come quick!" His voice echoed through the night. The ewe turned her head and stared at him, but didn't move.

Within moments he heard his friends approaching, followed by a the muffled sound of hooves against the grass and gentle baa-ing protests at being relocated so quickly. Seth came up on one side of him, and Benjamin on the other. Benjamin tugged at his sleeve. "What is it?"

"Look!" Jonathan pointed.

"I know. We saw it, too. We were already on our way to get you when we heard you call."

"Have you ever seen anything like it?"

"Have you ever seen anything like it?"
"Never. Something strange is going on here."

"Never. Something strange is going on here."

As if in response to his comment, the light from the star grew brighter, reaching down nearly to the earth at their feet, and began to take on a form—a being of light, so bright it nearly blinded them. Jonathan held up a hand to his eyes.

"Fear not," a voice said from the light. "I bring you good news of great joy for all people. For unto you is born this day in the city of David a Savior, the Messiah, Christ the Lord."

Jonathan felt his knees buckle, and he fell to the ground.

"You will find the child wrapped in swaddling clothes, and lying in a manger," the being went on. And then, without warning, the single being of light became a hundred, a thousand.

"Glory to God in the highest!" they said in unison, "And peace on earth to those who find favor with God!"

Then, as suddenly as they had come, they disappeared. Jonathan looked around and saw Seth and Benjamin, prone on the grass beside him. The sheep still stood a little ways off, grazing as if nothing unusual had happened.

"Did you see that?" Seth murmured. "Or am I dreaming?"

"If you're dreaming, we all had the same dream." Benjamin got up from the ground, a dazed expression on his face.

"Was it what I think it was?" Jonathan stammered. "An angel?" He stared at his friends. "Do you *believe* in angels?"

Benjamin shook his head as if to clear it. "I do now."

"All right, we're all agreed on what we saw. And that it was real."

Seth and Benjamin both nodded.

"So what do we do about it?"

"I guess we go into Bethlehem. That's what the angel said. A child, the Messiah, has been born, and it seems we're supposed to greet him."

Seth frowned. "But why us? If the Messiah has *really* come, after all these years, wouldn't his arrival be announced to someone a little more important than us? A bunch of *shepherds*?"

Jonathan cleared his throat. "Maybe. But I, for one, do not intend to stand around here arguing the point. I'm going to Bethlehem."

Benjamin took a step in Jonathan's direction. "Me, too. But how are we going to find him?"

"Look, I'm not exactly what you'd call a religious man," Jonathan said. "But I'd bet my flock that if the Messiah has finally arrived, other people besides us know about it. We go to Bethlehem and follow the crowds. It should be simple enough."

"You can stay here and watch the sheep if you want to, Seth," Benjamin muttered. "We'll be back later."

"Wait! You're not going to leave me here alone! If something is happening, I want to be in on it, too."

Jonathan puzzled for a moment, and then said, "All right. We'll all go. The sheep can fend for themselves." Even as the words came out, he couldn't believe he said them. No shepherd worth the name ever left his sheep alone—especially not on the edge of a deep ravine. Anything could happen. In a matter of seconds a wolf or lion could come down out of the hills and kill them all. They could wander over the cliff and kill themselves. At the very least, the shepherds would have to spend the next two days rounding them back up again.

But right now, none of that mattered. In unison, Seth and Benjamin nodded. "Let's go."

Together the three of them made their way across the hills into the tiny village of Bethlehem. When they reached the outskirts of the town, Seth shook his head. "Pretty poor place for a Messiah to be born in, wouldn't you say?"

"Keep quiet, will you? This way." Jonathan, now the acknowledged leader, moved toward the center of the village. When they came to what was obviously the town's only inn, he stopped. "This has to be the right place—Bethlehem isn't that big." He scratched his head, confused. "It's completely dark. Everybody's asleep."

Benjamin nodded. "This is odd. How can the Messiah be born and nobody pay any attention?"

"Wait a minute! Didn't the angel say something about the child lying in a *manger*? There must be a stable out back. Let's try there."

Jonathan led the way down a dark path to the back of the inn, then stopped short. "Look!" he breathed.

A faint, untraceable light filtered down directly over the little cave, illuminating the last twenty feet or so of the path. When they got to the door, Jonathan opened it cautiously and peered inside.

Surrounded by animals—a cow, a couple of sheep, and a gentle gray donkey—the young mother lay propped up on a bed of hay covered by a blanket. Beside her stood a large man, also young, but obviously strong, with wide shoulders and muscular arms. He took a step forward. "Shalom, friends. May I help you?"

In a stammering voice Jonathan related their experience on the hillside with the angels.

It sounded completely incredible, but the man did not show any sign of disbelief.

"Ah, I see," he said. He turned his head toward the woman, who smiled and motioned them inside. "I am Joseph. My wife's name is Mary."

It wasn't at all what Jonathan had expected. No heavenly light, no ethereal glow, no angels singing in the rafters. No worshipers, no dignitaries to welcome the Chosen One. Just an ordinary, rather small stable, occupied by a young girl, her husband, and her newborn child.

"But why, out of all the possibilities, did the angel come to us— a bunch of dirty shepherds, outcasts?"

But one look at the infant's countenance told Jonathan he was, indeed, in the right place. He knelt in the hay beside the makeshift bed and held out a finger to touch the baby's face. One tiny hand reached out and gripped his, and even as the tears fell, Jonathan found himself laughing.

"I see you've brought a friend with you," Joseph observed.

Jonathan looked around. There, at his side, was his wayward ewe. For once she had followed him, all the way to Bethlehem. She nudged him aside, found an empty stall, and began to eat.

"There's one thing I don't understand," Jonathan said after a while.

"Only one?" Joseph chuckled.

"Well, probably more than one," Jonathan agreed. "But why, out of all the possibilities, did the angel come to us—a bunch of dirty shepherds, outcasts? Why not to kings and princes and priests?"

The young mother, Mary, smiled. "Perhaps," she said softly, "the kings and princes and priests of this world do not see their need for a Savior. The outcasts do."

Jonathan thought about this, and finally he nodded. "The angel said there would be peace to those who have found favor with God. But I don't know if that includes us. I mean, I've never been very religious—"

"Maybe religion has little to do with God's favor," Mary suggested. "What does your heart tell you? Is your soul at peace?"

"More than it's ever been before," Jonathan answered honestly. "But I'm not sure why."

"*Why* is a question that rarely gets an answer," Mary mused. "What matters is how we respond to what we've been given. How it changes our lives for the better."

Jonathan nodded and fell silent. For a long time he sat there, watching the infant sleep, thinking about what had transpired this night. At last he turned to Seth and Benjamin. "It's almost dawn. I suppose we'd better go."

"Peace be upon you," Joseph said as he walked with them to the stable door. He smiled and looked down. " It appears you are taking a blessing with you."

Jonathan followed Joseph's gaze. His wandering ewe stood beside him, now considerably thinner, and next to her, a gangly newborn lamb. He chuckled, picked the lamb up, and rested it across his shoulders. "Thank you," he said, "for sharing this moment with us."

All the way back through Bethlehem, Jonathan and Seth and Benjamin stopped everyone they saw, telling them of the miracle that had happened. Most rushed on by, too busy with the work of the morning to pay them any mind. But no matter what the response, they told, and kept on telling.

When they got back to the ravine above the village, the entire flock was exactly where they had left them—healthy and unharmed, and all there, down to the last one. Jonathan set the new lamb down and watched as it followed unsteadily while its mother found a grazing spot.

Seth brought out bread and cheese, and the three of them ate breakfast together in silence. No one, it seemed, had anything to say.

Jonathan kept quiet, too, mulling over his own thoughts. No, it wasn't what he had expected, this birth announcement for the long-awaited Savior. Born in a barn, without fanfare or riches or worldwide fame. But it was right, somehow. A Messiah to the outcast, to the poor, to the homeless. To him.

He glanced aside and smiled as the newest addition to his flock nudged its mother for milk. Somehow he suspected that his wayward ewe wouldn't be wandering away so much anymore. And he was very certain that no matter how many years went by, he would never, ever forget the miraculous night when this lamb came into the world.

THE ANCIENTS

he old man awoke to find himself in that in-between time when darkness has not fully given way to dawn. He lay there and watched for a few minutes as the shapes around him, gray and shrouded, gradually, imperceptibly, began to take on form and color.

"Simeon," he muttered to himself as he lifted his aching body off the sleeping mat, "you need more rest. More rest." Perhaps he would not go to the temple this morning. He would say his prayers like a faithful son of Israel and save his rusty knees the walk into town.

Why, he wondered, did people sleep less and less as they grew older? It seemed to him that an ancient body would need more hours of restoration, not fewer. It was something he fully intended to speak to the Almighty about when the two of them came face to face. He hoped it would be soon.

He shuffled to the ewer and bowl that sat on a table at the edge of the room and splashed his face with cold water. *Soon*, he thought—a ritual morning prayer these past few years, as his body grew wearier and stiffer by the day. *Soon, O God of the Universe, Lord Almighty. Soon.*

Years ago, God had revealed to Simeon through the Spirit that he would not die until he had beheld the Messiah face to face. At the time, Simeon had thought himself the most blessed among men—he, after all, would live to see the Chosen One. But as the years dragged by and no Messiah was forthcoming, Simeon began to wonder. He never doubted the voice of the Almighty—God had spoken too clearly to allow for any misgivings. But he had begun to believe that the promise was an evidence of God's mysterious sense of humor: how long would the Lord have to keep him alive to see the prophecy fulfilled? As long as Methuselah—or longer?

Simeon dressed, draped his prayer shawl over his head, and went outside to present his morning litany. The sun was rising through broken clouds, and the air held a chill. He steeled himself against a shiver and began to pray: "Blessed art thou, Lord of the Universe, Creator of heaven and earth . . ."

Simeon halted, arrested by the incredible beauty of the sunlight shafting through the clouds over the bright white buildings of Jerusalem. It almost looked as if God were reaching out from the heavens, pointing down to the very place where he stood.

Then a voice whispered in his mind: *This is the day.*

"This is the day that the Lord has made; let us rejoice and be glad in it," Simeon murmured, continuing to pray as his mind progressed through the Psalm. "Blessed is the one who comes in the name of the Lord . . ."

This is the day, the voice repeated. *The One who comes in the name of the Lord comes today.*

"The Lord is God, and has given us light," Simeon persisted.

The Light has dawned, the voice whispered. *The new day is at hand. This is the day.*

Suddenly the truth pierced through to Simeon's mind. *This is the day. The Light has dawned.*

The One who comes in the name of the Lord comes today. His heart began to race, and despite the chill of the morning, a bead of sweat formed across his neck and trickled down his spine. *Today?*

He muttered a hurried "Omaine," trusted God to understand his haste, and rushed inside the house to retrieve his cloak. He had to get to the temple. Now.

When he reached the temple, a circumcision was already in progress. Simeon watched as a young girl and her powerfully-built husband presented their infant boy for the ritual. The girl, he noticed, turned her head aside when the cut was made, cringing when her son began

His heart began to race, and despite the chill of the morning, a bead of sweat formed across his neck and trickled down his spine.

to cry. The man stood silent and reverent, watching. When the ceremony was finished, the father scooped the tiny babe up in his massive arms and comforted him, then handed him to his mother.

Simeon smiled. A nice little family—obviously poor, but faithful. How it warmed his old heart to see the younger generation being true to their heritage, true to their God! He looked past them, his eyes scanning the temple for some sign of the Anointed One. He would no doubt be a person of some importance, easily recognizable . . .

Blessed is the One who comes in the name of the Lord.

Simeon frowned. Surely God could not mean the bawling infant of this poverty-stricken couple? He shook his head. No. *Blessed is the One who comes,* the voice repeated. *Blessed. Blessed.*

Well. This was not at all what Simeon had envisioned, but who was he to resist the nudging of the Spirit? He walked forward and looked down into the face of the child.

The baby had grown quiet, calmed by his mother's nearness. Tears still streaked his round little face, but his eyes opened in an expression of wonder. Without warning, Simeon's heart melted and he reached out a quivering hand toward the baby's head.

"His name is Jesus," the young mother said quietly. "Would you like to hold him?"

Simeon opened his arms and gathered the infant to his breast. At the first touch, a jolt went through him, like liquid warmth filling his veins and pumping strength and renewed faith into his heart. He lifted the baby up, and as tears coursed down his cheeks and lodged in his beard, Simeon began to speak:

"Lord, may your servant now depart in peace, according to your word. For my eyes have seen your salvation, prepared in the presence of all the people—a light to enlighten the Gentiles, and the glory of your people Israel."

He turned and saw the young couple standing by silently, their eyes wide. "The blessing of Almighty God be upon you," Simeon murmured. "This child is destined for the falling and rising of many in Israel, and as a sign to be opposed. The inner thoughts of many will be revealed by him, and a sword will pierce your own heart as well."

The girl stared at him. She could not know, not at this moment, what the years to come held for her and her son. Perhaps it was just as well. God had promised that Simeon would live to see the Messiah face to face. That promise had now been fulfilled. But for some reason he only vaguely understood, Simeon hoped above all hope that the promise did *not* include living to watch the child's future unfold.

For a long time Simeon stood there, able to say no more, until a gentle tug at his sleeve brought him back to the present. He turned to see a withered old face looking over his shoulder.

It was Anna, the prophetess. Older than Simeon—if such a thing were possible—she had served in the temple for more than seventy years. She had been married once, long ago, but only for a few short years, and ever after that had remained a widow. She stayed in the temple night and day. Most people thought her a little odd—she fasted and prayed and worshiped, and as far as he knew, had never set foot outside the temple doors. Simeon had never paid her much mind, but now, the expression in her eyes told him everything. She, too, had received a word from the Lord. And on this day, her promise also had been fulfilled.

She gazed first at the child, and then at Simeon. "He is the Promised One," she murmured. It was not a question.

Simeon nodded, placed the child in her arms, and stepped aside as Anna began to sing and worship God: "Hear, O Jerusalem, sing and be glad. Redemption has come this day to the house of Israel. . . ."

When the prophetess was finished, she handed the child back to his mother and wandered off into the temple. Simeon could hear her in the distance, speaking excitedly to everyone she passed, pointing back toward them and telling them that the Promise of the Ages had at long last been fulfilled. No one, it seemed, paid much attention to her words. She was just Anna, the crazy old woman who lived in the temple.

The young couple, still looking a bit dazed, took their son, received Simeon's blessing, and went to offer their sacrifice according to the law—a pair of turtle doves and two young pigeons. The poor man's offering.

All the way home Simeon thought about what he had seen this day. An ordinary infant, to all appearances, whom the hand of God had touched. The Messiah. The Chosen One. God's Anointed. It had finally happened.

He went into his house, removed his cloak, and lay down. He had to admit that he didn't feel quite so old anymore. His joints seemed to work a little better on the walk home, and he wasn't as winded by the time he reached his door. But still, he was tired—that wonderful, relaxing kind of tired that comes at the end of a fulfilling day.

Never again would he pray, *Soon, Lord. Soon.* From this day forth his prayer would be, *Thank you, Lord. Thank you.*

"Master, may your servant now depart in peace," he murmured. "For my eyes have seen your salvation . . ."

And then, before he could finish his thought, Simeon fell asleep.

aspar, can you still see the star?"

"Yes, Melchior. Right there——" He pointed, first to the charts spread out on the ground in front of him, and then to the star-studded sky.

Melchior squinted. His eyesight was failing him, especially at night, but he trusted Caspar's expertise when it came to reading the heavens. The youngest of their group, but with a wisdom that far exceeded his years, Caspar had been the one to keep them on track, to encourage them when their spirits flagged.

"I know my eyes aren't what they used to be, but isn't it growing dimmer?"

Caspar straightened up and nodded. "You're right. It is."

Melchior sighed. More than once during this long, tedious journey he had wondered if they might not be on a fool's errand. Now the star seemed to be fading—their only source of direction disappearing right before their eyes.

"But," Caspar went on in a positive tone of voice, "I don't think it will matter."

Balthasar came up behind him. "Don't think what will matter?"

"We're losing the star," Melchior muttered.

"But we're almost there," Caspar interjected. "Look at the charts I've prepared. The only

major city within the vicinity of the star is Jerusalem. We're seeking a king, aren't we? The king promised in the ancient scrolls? Well—" He slapped his hand down on the map and grinned. "Where else do you find a king but in a palace—in Jerusalem!"

Three days later, the entourage stood before King Herod. "Where do we find the one who is born King of the Jews?" Balthasar, the spokesman, inquired. "We have seen his star in the east and have come to worship him."

The king's face paled, and he excused himself for a hurried conference with his advisers. When he returned, he looked a little less panicked. "My priests and scribes have searched the holy scrolls. They tell me of an obscure prophecy that indicates that one called Messiah is to be born in Bethlehem of Judea. But—" He narrowed his eyes and fixed them with a steely gaze. "If I give you directions, you must promise to return this way and tell me what you have found." The king cleared his throat and smiled—a forced smile that did not reach his eyes. "If a king has been born in my provinces, I wish to go and do homage to him as well."

"Do you really think that snake has any intention of doing homage to a new monarch?" Caspar growled as they made their way out of Jerusalem and took the road that led to the little village of Bethlehem.

"It is doubtful that his intentions are honorable," Balthasar answered. "But we will keep our eyes open."

Much to their delight, the star reappeared, brighter than before, and at last they found the place—not in Bethlehem, but Nazareth, in a region known as Galilee. No palaces here, no impressive residences. Only a cluster of tiny huts and barns, and the overwhelming aura of poverty.

III

"Surely not," Melchior said.

"The stars do not lie," Caspar responded. "At least let's go inside and see what we find."

What they found was a small house just like all the others, barely more than a hovel. It was occupied by a carpenter named Joseph, his child-bride Mary, and a brown-eyed toddler. "Shalom," the man said when he opened the door. "Peace be unto you."

"And unto your household," Balthasar replied.

The man ushered them inside, offered them bread and wine, and graciously extended all the hospitality of his home to the travelers. Caspar exchanged glances with Melchior and Balthasar, and they nodded. It wasn't a king's palace, by any definition, but it was the right place.

"We have been led to you by a star shining in the east," Balthasar explained. "Our ancient texts prophesy of a king to come, whose birth would be marked by the brightest star in the firmament." He glanced down at the toddler, playing with a wooden spoon on the dirt floor. "The prophecies speak of an infant king born in Bethlehem, but the star led us here."

"He *was* born in Bethlehem," Joseph answered. "We had traveled there for the census, and stayed until Mary recovered her strength. After going to Jerusalem for his circumcision, we returned home to Nazareth. That was a year and a half ago."

Balthasar sighed. "It did take us a very long time to make the journey."

"We thank you for your trouble," the young mother said. Mary didn't seem in the least surprised to find a convoy of wealthy and influential magi sitting in her tiny house. "Our son's name is Jesus."

Following protocol, they knelt on the dirt floor next to the child. "Hail, King Jesus," they chanted. "We offer our gifts in honor of your birth. Gold, frankincense, and myrrh." Carefully they laid out their offerings, housed in elaborate and valuable treasure chests.

The child looked up at them and laughed, then awkwardly pried open the first box. His eyes lit up with glee as he inspected the contents, and his chubby hands reached in and began to scatter gold coins around the room.

Mary leaned over and laid a hand on his head. "That's enough, sweetheart." She looked

"Do they have any idea who their son is, or what is in store for him?" Melchior mused as they faced their caravan back toward Jerusalem.

up at the wise men. "I'll put these away. If he gets into the myrrh and frankincense, it wouldn't take him long to make a very sticky mess of the whole house."

All in all, it was a rather strange visit. For months on end Caspar, Melchior, and Balthasar had traveled day and night to get here, and then, before they knew it, the visit was over. Stifling a twinge of disappointment, they gathered their entourage, made their farewells, and began the long trek home.

"Do they have any idea who their son is, or what is in store for him?" Melchior mused as they faced their caravan back toward Jerusalem.

"Partially, I think," Balthasar answered. "They certainly showed no surprise at our arrival. But they treat him just like any other eighteen-month-old boy."

"He *is* an eighteen-month-old boy," Caspar said. "But did you see his face? There's something about him, something—"

"Something holy?" Balthasar supplied.

"Perhaps," Melchior hedged. "So did we, or did we not, fulfill our mission? Did we find the king whose coming was announced in the prophecies?" He gazed at the youngest among them and saw him smile. "Well, young Caspar, what is your answer? You look as if you had something on your mind."

Caspar nodded. "Balthasar, Melchior, you are my elders, and as such I will give you the respect due to you. But with your permission I will speak my mind."

Balthasar chuckled. "Speak on, young lion."

"We did what we were called to do. Does not the Holy One honor the faithfulness of those who obey? Perhaps what we discovered was different—quite different—than the image we held in our minds when we started out. We found no king, no ruler, no opulent palace. The child lives in poverty, with a carpenter for a father and girl for a mother." He paused and took a deep breath. "But now we have a choice—the same decision every individual faces. We can choose to embrace this as the work of the Divine, or we can disbelieve. My father taught me that a truly wise man looks not to the appearance of things, but to their substance. And I, for one, choose to believe that this child whose star we followed is, indeed, King of the Universe. I cannot prove it, but I feel the truth of it, deep inside. And in this case, I must trust my heart rather than my head."

Melchior opened his mouth to protest, but Balthasar interrupted him before he could speak.

"And what of your training, young Caspar? Were you not taught to question, to investigate, to search out the truth with diligence?"

"I *have* sought," Caspar responded, "and I have found. Not the answers to my questions, necessarily, but the source of all wisdom." He jutted out his chin. "And from this day forth, I will follow that wisdom wherever it may lead."

When they camped for the night, Melchior could not rid his mind of the echoes of young Caspar's newfound faith. For his own part, he wasn't so sure. He tossed and turned until the moon rose high, then fell into a shallow and restless sleep.

At dawn, he awoke feeling different, somehow, and unsure of the reason for the change. Then he remembered the dream. A being of light, shining like the sun, saying to him, *Return not to Jerusalem, nor to the court of Herod. For the king intends harm to the child. His life lies in your hands.*

"I had the same dream!" Balthasar confirmed as they prepared to set out. "The same dream exactly!"

Melchior stole a glance at Caspar, whose face bore an expression of wonder and awe. "Go ahead, say it."

"Say what, Melchior?" Caspar looked puzzled.

"Say, *I told you so.*"

"I only told you the conclusion that I had reached," Caspar answered. "Your perspectives are your own."

They turned the caravan around and headed home by a different route. Caspar said little, and Balthasar remained silent as well, leaving Melchior to his own thoughts.

Was it an angel, that being who came to him in his sleep? Had he, indeed, discovered the Messiah of the prophecies in a lowly hovel in Galilee? Would his life be changed forever by this brief and strange encounter?

Melchior found no resolution to his dilemma. He still had questions, hundreds of them. But of one thing he was absolutely certain:

He would do it again. Despite the hardship, the interminable journey, the uncertainties— whatever the cost, if he had it to do over again, he would follow that star to the ends of the earth and back.

Perhaps true wisdom, after all, lay not in the finding, but in the willingness to seek. Not in gaining answers, but in taking risks.

oseph tossed and turned, trying to be quiet so as not to wake Mary, but unable to settle down and sleep. Seldom in his life had he experienced the frustration of sleeplessness. He had always worked hard, and at the end of the day he reveled in the satisfying tiredness that came with a job well done. When the lamp went out, Joseph slept, and woke refreshed with each new dawn.

Only twice in recent memory had he lain awake until the early hours of morning: in Bethlehem, the night their son was born, and nine months before that, those few days of agony before the angel had appeared to him in a restless dream, instructing him to take Mary as his wife.

Was God trying to tell him something now?

Joseph got up and tiptoed away from the bed. Mary stirred slightly, mumbled in her sleep, and then began to snore softly once again. He passed by his son's little bed—the boy had long since outgrown the cradle Joseph had made—and looked down at the chubby face. In sleep, the child looked serene and peaceful. Quite a difference from the energetic toddler who kept both of them running from daylight till dark.

The lad's eyes opened, and he reached his arms up.

"Abba!"

Joseph reached down and caressed his head. "Yes, my son," he soothed. "Abba's here. Go back to sleep, now."

But Jesus would not be dissuaded. "Abba!" he insisted.

"All right, all right." Joseph lifted Jesus out of his crib, wrapped him in his blanket, and took him over near the fire. Holding the boy in one arm, he stirred the embers of the fire and put on a little more wood. The flames danced to life, reflecting in the child's dark eyes. When the fire was burning, Joseph sat down in a chair and began to rock.

"Let the redeemed of the Lord say so," he sang softly, "whom God has delivered from the hands of their enemies . . ." Jesus's eyelids began to droop. His hand grasped Joseph's finger, and within a few moments his breathing grew even.

Why, Joseph wondered, *can I not sleep in peace even as he does?* Was it because of the money, the treasures brought by the wise men who had come to do homage to the child? It wasn't a fortune, exactly, but it was far more than Joseph had ever possessed. And with money came increased responsibility—and, perhaps, a few sleepless nights.

But he didn't think so. He and Mary had already agreed that the gifts should be saved for the future, for the uncertainties that could not be anticipated. In the meantime, their lives would go on in the simplicity they were accustomed to. Joseph would continue his carpentry, the work he loved so much. They would stay in Nazareth. Nothing would change.

The heat of the fire seeped into his bones, and the warmth from Jesus's little body soaked into his chest. Joseph found his own eyes growing heavy, but still he sat there, holding his son, staring into the flames.

"Take the child and his mother, and flee to Egypt, and remain there until I tell you."

The voice startled Joseph, and he looked around. The house was dark, the fire a little dimmer, and he still held the sleeping child in his arms. Had he imagined it? He strained his ears, but all he heard was the gentle crackling of the flames.

"Take the child and his mother, and flee to Egypt, and remain there until I tell you," the voice repeated. *"For Herod is about to search for the child, to destroy him."*

An image passed before Joseph's eyes—the King standing on a dais as his soldiers paraded by with the naked sons of his neighbors and friends impaled upon their swords. The soldiers were waving the infant bodies like triumphal flags, and Herod was laughing. A gruesome, horrible scene . . .

Joseph awoke with a start. The fire had died, and he was shivering. What a blood-chilling, terrifying dream! He shook his head to try to rid himself of the memory, but still it remained.

This was no ordinary nightmare. It was a warning.

He clutched little Jesus tighter to his chest, and the boy stirred in protest and began to whine.

"Joseph?" Mary sat up on the sleeping mat and pushed her hair out of her eyes. "Is everything all right?"

He wanted to reassure her, to say, *Yes, Mary, everything's fine; go back to sleep.* But everything wasn't fine, and he knew it. Crazy as it seemed, there was only one thing to do.

"Get up, Mary." He went to her and laid his son on the sleeping mat beside her.

"It isn't daylight yet, is it?" she mumbled. "Come back to bed."

119

"No, it's still dark. But we have to leave—now!" As he moved about the house, lighting lamps and gathering supplies, Joseph told her about the message that had come in his dream. "Herod is going to try to kill our son, and we can't let that happen."

In an instant, Mary was on her feet. She dressed, threw extra clothes into a bag, and packed bread, wine, and cheese for the journey. "Egypt?" she repeated. "We're going to Egypt? But how will we live?"

"We'll manage. God will provide, and—"

He heard a crash, and turned. Jesus, now wide awake, sat in the center of a cache of gold coins, playing with them and laughing. Somehow he had toddled over to the table, climbed up on it, and pulled down from a shelf the small chest Balthasar had brought to honor the child.

Joseph grinned. "It looks as if God has *already* provided."

"The gifts! I had almost forgotten!"

He nodded. "I didn't think of them, either. But God didn't forget."

By the time dawn broke, Joseph, Mary, and Jesus were well into the hills of Judea and making their way south and east toward Egypt. An extended journey lay ahead of them, days of camping in the desert, taking refuge in towns along the way. But at least they had enough money to sustain them. They would make it—Joseph believed that with all his heart. And someday, when it was safe to return, they would come home again.

A rumbling in the valley below arrested Joseph's attention. "Look!" he told Mary, and nodded at the scene below them. "Herod's soldiers, hundreds of them, on horseback, coming from Jerusalem!"

Mary shifted on the donkey's back and gripped Jesus in her arms. "I didn't think it would happen so quickly. We got out just in time."

They stood there staring, watching until the King's troops vanished in a cloud of dust.

But little Jesus didn't notice the soldiers. He had eyes only for the morning. "Abba!" he squealed, jabbing a chubby finger toward the east. "Pretty!"

The sun was rising into a bank of clouds, painting the eastern sky with a panorama of color—red, gold, purple, blue. One shaft of sunlight pierced the clouds, directing them, it seemed, toward Egypt.

Joseph scooped his son off the donkey's back and held him close. "Abba!" the child repeated, pointing to the sun.

"Abba," Joseph echoed. The Father who loved them and protected them. The Parent who watched over them all, provided for their needs, gave them direction. The God who would never forsake them.

"Yes," he repeated. "Abba is here."

Then he settled his son on the donkey with Mary, and they began the long trek toward Egypt.

emetrius leaned on the edge of the well in the center of the little village of Bethlehem and shut his eyes against the carnage. Blood ran between the cracks of the cobblestones, stained his boots, dripped from the edge of his own sword. He had fought in many battles and come forth victorious. He was a servant of the King, a Centurion, a warrior accustomed to spilling the blood of his enemies.

But never like this.

When Herod had called his captains and given the order, the King was furious, raving about being deceived by some wise men who were supposed to report back to him on the location of some pretender to the throne. Apparently the sages were wiser than Herod had counted on; they had escaped Judea and vanished. And now, since Herod could not find the exact identity and location of the usurper, he had determined to eliminate any possibility of a new king rising up to take his place.

Like all the other Centurions, Demetrius had been outraged. Such treason was punishable by death. He would find this traitor, track him down and run a spear through his heart. Anything to protect and serve his King.

Then Herod revealed the rest of the story, and Demetrius could not believe his ears.

Children? Babies? Yes, he had heard right. Throughout Judea and Galilee, any male child under the age of two was to be sought out and exterminated, the way Herod's personal guards would exterminate rats in the palace garbage. That, the King had declared smugly, would solve the problem once and for all.

Demetrius and some of the other captains had discussed the matter privately, out of earshot of the King's spies. The man must be mad, they concluded. He would have to be insane to order the annihilation of hundreds of helpless infants! How could they obey such a maniacal command?

But in the end, Demetrius, like the others, *had* obeyed. At this very moment, troops were fanning out into every town and village from Jerusalem to Nazareth. Mothers were screaming. Fathers were fighting. Rabbis were praying. But none of the resistance would have any effect. Herod's will would be done.

He could rationalize his actions, of course. He had a wife to support, and two sons—a two-year-old and a newborn. His position as a Centurion was an honorable one. He had a job to do. He was only following orders.

Still, logic could not quell the nausea that rose up in his throat, or diminish the cold sweat that broke out across his face. Demetrius kept seeing his own precious children, Artemis and Julius, speared on the point of a sword. He could hear his dear wife Claudia screaming, imagine the expression of horror on her face. . . .

He had to stop thinking like this. Had to look at this assignment as a job, like all the others. Had to, somehow, see these dead babies as enemies of the realm. Orders were orders, and a soldier—if he wanted to live—did what he was told.

At the moment, however, Demetrius wasn't sure he wanted to live.

Weary beyond imagining, he hauled a bucket of water from the well, splashed his face, and tried to wash the dried blood from the blade of his sword. The chaos had subsided, and most of the parents had gone into their homes to mourn in private. On one side of the square, a rough wooden cart was piled high with tiny naked bodies.

"Sir?"

A young recruit stood before him, a brawny lad with a barrel chest and huge, muscular forearms. But his face was pale and had a greenish cast, and his eyes held a haunted look. The voice, when it came again, was shaky and hoarse. "Sir, we're finished here."

Demetrius stared at him. "What?"

"We're finished. Everything is . . . uh, done." He gestured with a trembling hand toward the cart.

Demetrius shuddered. "Put a cover over that thing. Blankets, anything." After the soldiers cleared out, the grieving parents would come to claim their children's bodies. But for now, he couldn't bear to look at it.

"Yes, sir." The lad turned to go, then apparently had second thoughts. "Sir?" he said as he looked back at his commander. "I don't mean to question orders, sir, but was this . . . was this really *necessary?*"

Demetrius looked up at the fresh-faced young soldier. "The King commanded it," he responded.

"Yes, sir."

The boy left, and Demetrius sank to the edge of the well, unable to move. The young soldier's question echoed his own misgivings, but he didn't dare give an honest answer to the lad's question. No, it wasn't necessary. It was madness.

He heard a noise, and turned. An old man with a long gray beard, dressed in the garb of a

He looked down at his own hands, stained brown with the blood of innocents.

127

Jewish priest, was walking slowly through the square. His face was covered with ashes, and as he walked, he tore his clothes and cried out: "A voice is heard in Ramah, wailing and loud lamentation! Rachel is weeping for her children, refusing to be comforted, because they are no more!"

The ancient priest then launched into the Kaddish, the Jewish prayer for the dead. How many times this day had Demetrius heard those words? Prayer to a god who could not, or would not, lift a hand to stop the slaughter.

He looked down at his own hands, stained brown with the blood of innocents. Was it truly the failing of their god, that this terrible tragedy had happened? Despite their losses, these Jews believed. They still prayed. They did not blame their deity for what Herod—and Demetrius himself—had done.

It was time to leave, to gather his troops and ride back to Jerusalem. But Demetrius couldn't move. He felt as if he were nailed to this spot, this insignificant little village called Bethlehem.

The priest wandered by and gazed at him with sad eyes. "Peace be to you," he mumbled.

Peace? Would Demetrius ever find peace again? Would he ever rid his mind of the living nightmare he had endured today?

The old man shrugged. "Messiah is one your swords cannot destroy. He will rise with healing in his wings."

He grabbed the old man by the sleeve. "Rabbi," he asked urgently, "why do you keep on praying?"

"It will not always be this way," the rabbi answered cryptically. "When Messiah comes, he will free us from bondage and give us new life."

"Who is this Messiah?" Demetrius demanded. "Is he the one King Herod sought to kill? I must know!"

The old man shrugged. "Messiah is one your swords cannot destroy. He will rise with healing in his wings." He shuffled away, still praying.

All the way back to Jerusalem, Demetrius pondered the old rabbi's words. *He will rise with healing in his wings.* By the time the great temple came into view, he felt more at peace with himself than he ever thought possible. *I do not know your name, God of the Jews*, he prayed silently, *but I seek your forgiveness. Never again will I turn my sword against the innocent. And I ask that one day I might meet this Messiah, this Anointed One you have promised to send.*

In the palace of Herod the Great, Demetrius made his report before the King and managed, with some difficulty, to refrain from speaking his mind about the insanity of the command. Herod listened, nodding, and smiled at his son, young Herod Antipas, who stood by his side.

"You see, my son," he said, "our fine, brave soldiers have carried out your father's will. Now, when you are grown and sit upon this throne, you will never have to worry about some upstart who claims to be King of the Jews."

Demetrius saluted the king and departed from Herod's court. He was still a Centurion, still a soldier. But now he was also a seeker. And despite the King's grand words, Demetrius suspected that one day the "upstart" would show his face again—as the Messiah promised by the Jewish God.

He only hoped he lived to see that day, to meet the One whom Herod's swords could not destroy.

FIRST MARTYR

adassah sat in the window of the small hovel she shared with her husband Enos and looked out. Her eyes took in the red glow of the sunset, but her soul refused to give thanks for its beauty. She would never again see the color red without thinking of this day. This day of blood, when the streets ran red with the slaughter of Israel's sons.

The house was quiet, and in the distance she could hear the keening wail of the other mourners. Mothers like herself, whose breasts still swelled with milk for a child who would never nurse again. Fathers like Enos, who would never see his son stand in the temple and declare, "Today I am a man."

The setting sun proclaimed the start of the Sabbath, but Hadassah had no heart for worship. Enos had recovered the limp, lifeless form of her baby, her only son Jesse, and taken him away to be buried. He had urged her to come with him, to mourn at their child's graveside, to say her final farewells. But her wooden limbs would not support her; grief had drained her energy and sapped her strength. She couldn't even weep.

It had to be done now, Enos said, for according to the Law there could be no burial on the Sabbath. Hadassah snorted in disgust. The Law? What good was the Law? What good was it to be God's chosen if the Almighty would let a thing like this happen? Where had God been when Herod had raised the sword against her child—against every son of Israel under the age of two?

Her heart froze at the blasphemy, but her mind pressed on. All her life she had been a faithful daughter of Sarah, keeping the Law, holding the hope of Messiah in her heart. When Jesse had come, that tiny miracle of life and love, she had even believed that he might turn out to be the fulfillment of the prophecies. But what had her faithfulness gained her? An empty lap; a full breast with no infant son to suckle.

Dusk closed in as the sun dropped below the horizon. Enos would be returning soon, expecting to find her preparing the Sabbath meal. But she could not go on as if nothing had happened. She would sit here at the window, in the dress stained with Jesse's blood, until the Almighty gave her an answer to her questions.

How could God, who claimed to love her, allow the death of her only son? And such a violent death, impaled on the sword of Herod's soldier. The Almighty could not possibly understand what such a vision did to a mother's heart.

But I do understand, a voice whispered in the darkness.

Hadassah jerked upright and turned, peering into the dim recesses of the house. She saw nothing, but she felt it. A presence. Someone, close by.

"Who's there?" Her voice, tight with fear, trembled as she spoke.

It is I. I am.

Hadassah shook her head. In her grief and anguish, was she going mad, hearing things that were not there?

The words came again. *I understand.*

Hadassah's pulse pounded in her ears. For all her anger at the injustice of Jesse's death, she still believed. Her heart would not let her disbelieve. God had spoken in the past—not only to kings and prophets, but once in a while, to ordinary people like herself. No one could see the face of the Almighty and live, the Torah warned, but Hadassah was willing to take that risk. What did her life mean anyway, now that her son had been murdered?

Hadassah shook her head.

In her grief and anguish, was she going mad,

hearing things that were not there?

She tilted her head and raised her chin. "How can you understand?" she challenged. "You are not a mother."

I am, the voice murmured. *I am Mother and Father. I am the Beginning and the End. I am the Source and Culmination. I am Love.*

"Love?" Hadassah spat out. "What kind of love is this, that you stand by without intervening while my son and hundreds of others babies are put to the sword?"

There is a purpose, the voice said, *beyond anything you can imagine.*

"Purpose?" Hadassah hissed. "What purpose can there be in the death of an innocent? My son was barely a year old; he had not even begun to live his life." Rage swelled her chest, and she turned back to the window. "I *believed* in you," she spat out. "I lived according to the Law, and in hope of the Messiah. But the law is meaningless, and Messiah is a myth. And until *you* lose your only son to a violent and unjust death, do not talk to me about understanding, or about love!"

The whisper came again, and Hadassah thought, just for a moment, that the voice sounded choked, as if the speaker were fighting back tears: *I will lose my Son. It is done already. Your child was not the Chosen One, but there is a purpose in his life . . . and in his death. Look.*

Hadassah, still staring out the window, gazed toward the far horizon. The setting sun left a reflection, a scarlet backdrop, against the sky. Silhouetted against the red afterglow, she could make out a cluster of figures: a man, leading a donkey, and a woman riding, holding a bundle in her arms. A baby.

Behold the Lamb of God, who takes away the sins of the world, the voice said quietly.

Hadassah blinked and looked again. "How did this child escape the slaughter?" she demanded. "King Herod's order was clear—all male children under the age of two were put to death. Their blood still stains the streets of this village."

His time was not yet come, the voice murmured. *Jesse—your Jesse—took his place.*

As Hadassah watched, the scene on the horizon shifted. Now three crosses rose against the crimson sky, and an ethereal light surrounded the one in the center.

My Son will also die, the voice continued, *but not yet. His death will be your life, and the life of your child.*

Hadassah closed her eyes to block out the vision of the execution. The Lamb of God, the voice had said. The ultimate offering—not only for her, but for the entire world. And Jesse, her firstborn, had paved the way for Messiah.

Tears sprang to her eyes and coursed down her cheeks. A lump clogged in her throat and she couldn't speak. The pain was still there, but something more than the pain. Hope.

My tears were the first to fall when Jesse died, the voice said, quieter now, as if from a great distance. *I weep with you, as you shall weep with me. But the tears will subside and morning will bring victory. When you say Kaddish for your son, remember my Son as well. . . .*

Then the voice was gone. But the presence remained—no longer outside of her, in the room, but within, warming her and releasing the tears of anger and grief. For a long time Hadassah wept, but when her tears were spent and her rage dispelled, she could feel something else. Jesse. Close to her heart, a nearness so real that she could never again deny the truth.

He lived.

Not here, with her, but somewhere else. His life did have meaning. His death did have purpose. In some way she could not understand, he had died so that Messiah could live on. And one day Messiah would bring life to them all. A new life. A different kind of life.

Hadassah rose, changed into a clean dress, and lit the candles for the Sabbath meal. Enos would be home soon. They would begin the Shiva, the seven days of mourning. And together they would say Kaddish, for the son who had died and the One who was yet to give his life.

135

abriel took his accustomed place next to the throne and put an arm around the young boy who stood beside him. Behind them, innumerable thousands gathered—silent, waiting.

"Why is it so quiet, Gabriel?" the lad whispered.

"It is time."

"Time for what?"

"Time for the universe to witness the Creator's greatest wonder."

The boy frowned. "But I thought the *Birth* was the greatest wonder. You know, the Holy One becoming flesh, living among humans—"

"Keep silence, Jesse." Gabriel smiled to soften the reprimand. "Watch."

Jesse watched—they all watched—as the heavens opened to reveal a scene unlike any that had ever been witnessed or imagined. A hill, darkened by clouds that overshadowed the noon-day sun. A man, beaten and bloody, dragging himself up the slope to the top, where Roman soldiers waited with spikes and sledge hammers. And then a noise—a terrible ringing that echoed throughout earth and heaven. The blood-chilling sound of hammer striking nails.

"Who is he?" Jesse whispered in Gabriel's ear. "And why are they killing him?"

"I'm surprised you don't recognize him," Gabriel responded quietly. "He is the one you saved."

"The Holy Child?" Jesse shuddered. "It can't be! He wasn't supposed to die! I died so that he could live. You told me so!"

"That is true." Gabriel nodded. "But that was another time, Jesse. He has lived out the course of his days. He has given the world an example of God-centered living unlike anything the universe has ever seen. And now he dies, to open the doors of eternal life to all who will enter."

"It's not possible," Jesse protested. "He's grown man. I'm still a young boy."

"It *is* possible," Gabriel explained in a whisper. "Time for us is not like time for them. On earth, humans count days and weeks, months and years as if each event were separate, parading past them like rows of marching soldiers. As you grow, you'll come to understand that in eternity, all things are complete and entire. We know no present or past or future. Everything is one in God, whom we worship and serve. All is woven into one great timeless knot of love."

"Then what I am seeing has already happened?"

"In a manner of speaking."

"It doesn't look like love to me," Jesse stated flatly.

Gabriel squeezed the boy's shoulder. "Perhaps not. Love takes many forms—some of them readily recognizable, others hidden behind a divine, inscrutable purpose. Trust me, Jesse. Trust the Almighty One. This is love, in its grandest, most terrible incarnation."

"But what does it *mean?*" Jesse demanded. "What purpose can this possibly serve?"

"Keep watching."

The sky grew darker, and the earth shuddered under the burden of this death. A cry rose up, faint at first, then gathering momentum until it filled the universe with its force: *"My God, my God, why have you forsaken me?"*

Jesse covered his ears, and tears began to roll down his cheeks. "Why doesn't somebody *do something?*" he wailed. "Why doesn't somebody *help him?*

"Everything is one in God, whom we worship and serve. All is woven into one great timeless knot of love."

139

"No tears, now," Gabriel rebuked him gently. "There are no tears in heaven, remember? No pain, no regret."

"I can't help it," Jesse answered in a strangled voice. "I don't understand this."

"I don't fully understand it either. I only know what the Almighty has revealed—that this death is the key to eternal life."

"I don't like it," Jesse countered. "It seems so—unnecessary. I'm here, and others are, too. None of us lived to see this terrible moment, and yet here we are, already received into the Presence."

Gabriel smiled and shook his head gently. "You're thinking in human terms again, lad. In terms of time and space. Look around you. Who do you see?"

Jesse's eyes scanned the crowds, but he said nothing.

Gabriel pointed. "Over there, the prophets and sages. Moses and Miriam, Joshua. Elijah, Enoch, Noah. Abraham and Sarah. Isaiah. Esther and Deborah. Ruth, who claimed God's people as her own. Next to her, Rahab the Harlot, who risked her life to protect God's people. The Wise Ones who followed the star and worshiped Jesus when he was still a child. The shepherds, first to hear the good news. The Forerunner, Jesus' cousin John, beheaded by Herod. What do they all have in common?"

The boy shrugged.

"They were seekers of truth," Gabriel prompted. "They pursued the way of God, placed their faith in the hands of the Almighty, even though they had no idea exactly what they were waiting for, seeking for, hoping for."

"And now?" Jesse asked. "What about those who are alive on earth now, and the millions who will follow them?"

Gabriel smiled. "For them, for all, the fulfillment of the promise has come."

"But how can anyone comprehend the meaning of this moment?" Jesse frowned. "What about—what about—?"

"Your family?"

The boy gulped back his tears. "Yes. I worry about them. It's always the ones who are left behind who have the harder time of it."

"Look closer."

Jesse narrowed his eyes and peered at the scene. "Is that my mother, kneeling in the dirt? And my father, standing with his hands on her shoulders? Do they know why I had to die? Do they understand what is happening now?"

Gabriel thought about the question for a moment. "Your mother, Hadassah, knows in her heart but has no words for her faith. Your father, Enos, accepts what she has told him but cannot yet grasp the meaning. In time, everything will be clear to them, as it will be for you."

"And that is enough?"

Gabriel smiled. "The Almighty does not devise ways to exclude those who search after truth. God sees the heart, knows the deep longings of the spirit. And Jesus himself said it: All who seek will find their soul's desire."

The clouds grew darker, blocking out the last remnants of the sun. Thunder rumbled. The earth shook to its core. Once more, the voice rang out: *"It . . . is . . . finished."* And then, a light began to gather near the top of the cross, take shape, and rise up from the earth.

"It looks like a star!" Jesse breathed.

"Yes, a star," Gabriel agreed. "The star which fell to earth so many years ago now rises to its place again. The miracle has been accomplished."

As the star ascended higher and higher, all heaven broke forth in songs of praise: *"Hallelujah! Glory to God in the Highest, and peace to all on earth."*

Gabriel drew Jesse to his side and held him close. "What you see, young Jesse, is the fulfillment of a miracle which began an eternity ago in the heart of God. Because of your death, he survived. And because of his life—and his death—countless others will live eternally."

"Including my parents?"

"They have already begun," Gabriel assured him. "Faith looks beyond death. Faith hopes. Faith trusts, even when it does not know the outcome of its trust."

"This is a great miracle," Jesse whispered. "And what a wonder, that I have been part of it!"

A tear traced down the lad's cheek. And this time Gabriel did not rebuke him, for even in heaven, tears of joy are always welcome.

142